Electric Smoker Cookbook

Electric
Smoker
Cookbook

Electric Smoker Recipes, Tips, and Techniques to Smoke Meat like a Pitmaster

Hank Dunn

Would you like a healthy salad with that?

Enjoy a full week of fresh, healthy salad recipes. A new salad for every day of the week!

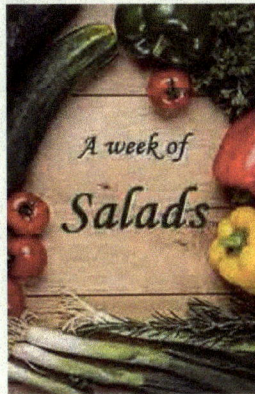

Grab this bonus recipe ebook *free* as our gift to you:

http://salad7.hotbooks.org

Contents

How I Became the Local "Pitmaster"........................ 9

Introduction to Barbeque 10

Introduction to Electric Smokers........................... 27

Pork Recipes.. 33

Beef Recipes.. 51

Poultry Recipes....................................... 67

Seafood Recipes 79

The "Dirty Dozen" and "Clean 15"....................... 91

Measurement Conversion Tables........................... 92

Recipe Index.. 93

How I Became the Local "Pitmaster"

I'm the kind of guy who always looks for good BBQ no matter where I go. I love brisket, pulled pork, dry rubs, sticky sauces, and everything else. I've tried to replicate my favorite flavors with a grill, but it doesn't get close. The grill is just too hot, and doesn't allow for that "low and slow" classic BBQ flavor that the experts talk about. Without a smoker, getting that melt-in-your-mouth brisket and exceptional smoked chicken just isn't possible.

Folks who have been to my cookouts always ask me "Hank, what do you recommend for smoking meat?" They say they want a smoker that is easy to use and doesn't require a lot of experience. "Well," I tell 'em, "for my money *you just can't beat an electric smoker.*" Personally I like the Masterbuilt brand, but there's lots of great electric smoker brands out there on the market, each with different models and options. I'd say if you're looking to smoke some meat for parties and big groups, you'll want to choose a big one. A 30-inch smoker with a window should do it. It's handy to be able to see the meat cooking without opening it up and disturbing the smoking process. I also recommend a model that has very precise temperature controls, because that's really important for BBQ. You might pay a pretty penny for her, but I'd rather have a really good smoker that lasts a long time than a cheap one that produces inferior food and breaks down after frequent use.

I remember when I was new to electric smoking. I wasn't very confident at first. For folks who are new to doing their own real BBQ, it can be intimidating cooking with all that smoke. I learned pretty quickly that smoking is actually easy! The smoker provides constant heat, so you don't need to worry about much, or be stuck babysitting the smoker for hours on end. I could even start it in the morning before going to work, leave it all day, and come back to an awesome dinner. All I'd have to do is whip up some coleslaw, cornbread, or whatever sides I feel like.

The electric smoker makes it hard to really mess things up too badly. Back when I was still pretty green I went ahead and hosted an office party where I got to really use my Masterbuilt's full capacity. People were shocked that it wasn't catered, and I felt pretty proud of myself. After that day I went from being simply a BBQ lover to earning the reputation as the local "Pitmaster"!

Now that I've been smoking for a while I've learned a thing or two, and developed a bunch of my own recipes along the way. All my favorites are right here in this cookbook. I really hope you and your folks like the information and recipes that I've put down here in this book. I'd be honored if you'd share your opinion with me, whether that be on Amazon, Goodreads, or if you happen to see me around town. I always love to hear from a fellow local "pitmaster"!

Git 'er done!
Hank Dunn

Introduction to Barbeque

When you hear the word "barbeque," what do you think of? Do you think of cooking outdoors on a grill? Maybe making the family some hot dogs, hamburgers, and vegetables? The "true" definition of BBQ is a little bit different, and it's been debated hotly for centuries. In 1830, Noah Webster (of the Webster Dictionary) defined "barbeque" as a verb that means, "to dress and roast a hog whole; to roast any animal whole." According to that definition, only meat can be truly barbequed, and it must be whole. Most people would say that is too limiting.

WHAT IS "BARBEQUE" EXACTLY?

Roasting a whole animal, specifically a pig, was the BBQ standard for many years in America. From colonial America through the Civil War, people would gather for barbecues. A slave was usually the pitmaster, and would spit-roast the whole pig over a large stack of logs. In 1844, fourteen years after Noah Webster's definition, one of America's first cookbooks contained a recipe for "Barbecue Shoat," which is hog. It was one of the first printed recipes with "barbeque" included. Most early cookbooks called any meat with a sauce "barbeque."

A whole pig, something that's spit-roasted, or anything with sauce - what's really BBQ? There are so many kinds of BBQ, like the traditional Southern style, Caribbean, Mongolian, and Korean. Most people would agree barbeque definitely includes more than pork. Generally, it seems that all BBQ must include at least one trait - smoke. When a food is cooked low and slow, with the presence of smoke, that's what makes it barbeque. If you're going to be a bit more specific, BBQ will be cooked with indirect heat in some kind of pit between 225-250 degrees. This results in extremely tender, fall-of-the-bone meat, no matter what kind of cut it is.

BARBEQUE AROUND THE COUNTRY

Barbeque is different depending on where you are in the USA. The major spots are North Carolina, Texas, Memphis, and Kansas City.

North Carolina (Eastern)

In the Eastern part of North Carolina, a pork shoulder or whole pig will be cooked with hickory smoke. When it's done, it gets chopped up or pulled into shreds, and mixed into a vinegar-based BBQ sauce. There's no tomato sauce. To serve, the meat goes on a bun with coleslaw.

North Carolina (Western)

Instead of pork shoulder, it's the pork butt that gets smoked. The other major distinction is that the vinegar sauce is made with tomato.

Texas

While North Carolina has its pork, Texas has beef. BBQ is a beef brisket smoked with oak or mesquite. They aren't big on sauce, either, but if you do have it, it's just ketchup mixed with meat drippings, some chili powder, and cumin.

Memphis

Shredded pork and ribs are the BBQ of choice in Memphis, Tennessee. You can get ribs "dry" or "wet." Dry means without sauce, while wet means you want to sauce it up with something tangy and sweet.

Kansas City

When Northerners think of BBQ, KC BBQ is usually what they picture. Kansas City is all about the sauce. Spare ribs are slathered generously, while there's also the fancy crispy "burnt ends," which are made from beef brisket.

THE HISTORICAL AND CULTURAL IMPACT OF BARBEQUE

Barbeque has an ancient and complex history. It's had its share of exploitation and tragedy. The first thing to know is that slow-cooking and smoking exist in every culture. In China, historians believe people had special kitchen devices for smoking meat, while in Japan and India, ceramic urns were used to cook food over coals. However, barbeque as the USA knows it originated with the clash between Spanish explorers and native tribes.

The Spanish meet BBQ

When the Spanish arrived in the Caribbean, Central America, and South America, they found a cooking device. The Taino Indian word sounded like "barbacoa" to the Spanish, which is where "barbeque" eventually came from. What exactly "barbacoa" meant is lost to history, and it appears to have had multiple meanings, including the cooking device, food that was cooked in it, a shelter, and even a bed.

The barbacoa was used for drying and smoking everything from fish to birds to deer. The meat was then salted and dried into jerky, and eaten in stews. It was very different from what we think of as "barbeque." The Spanish brought back this new style of cooking to Europe, and then took it to North America.

BBQ and race

Slaves taken to the colonies from the Caribbeans also brought their BBQ techniques and staples, including the hot red pepper. This history of BBQ and slavery being interwoven continued since slaves were usually the ones who roasted whole hogs with spits over a fire. Michael Pollan, author of Cooked: A Natural History of Transformation, says that BBQ is a black contribution to American culture.

By the time the 19th century came around, pork was essential to the BBQ cuisine of the American South. This is purely because there were so many pigs. Cornbread also emerged as the ideal side choice, because of how much corn there was. Corn grew better in the humid cultures than wheat. Other sides included sweet potatoes and fried okra. Because of how BBQ is perfect for turning cheap cuts of meat into tender eats, the poorest class - which were the Southern blacks - ate BBQ in the largest amounts.

In the first half of the 20th century, African-Americans moved up North, and brought BBQ with them. In the 1950's, BBQ spots owned by blacks were extremely prevalent, and "soul food" as we know it - fried chicken, okra, cornbread, hush puppies - went mainstream. Despite this link with race, BBQ transcends the color of people's skin, too. Even when race relations were bad, white people would still visit black-owned establishments for BBQ. In the South, with all its division, BBQ has also brought people together.

Barbeque elevated

Where is BBQ today? It's everywhere. It used to be seen as something that could fill your belly, but wasn't really an art form in the way other food styles were. Now, that's changed, and a city can't hope to be on the culinary map unless it has good BBQ. In 2015, a pitmaster ended up on the nomination list for the James Beard award (Best Chef: Southwest), the most sought-after title in cooking. He won, and at the reception, Aaron Franklin carved up smoked brisket served with crustless white beard and his famous espresso BBQ sauce.

BUILDING THE PERFECT BBQ

How do you pick a smoker? What's the difference between the main types? This section describes the types of smokers you have to choose from, the other accessories and equipment you might need, how to smoke meat even if you don't have a smoker, how to choose the right wood, and classic BBQ rub and sauce recipes. When you know these basics, you're on your way to becoming a great BBQ chef.

Types of smokers

When it comes to the device you use to smoke meat, you have lots of options. There are eight types: smoke box, propane, upright drum, vertical water, offset, trench, and electric.

Smoke box

Known as a smoke box or box smoker, these devices are what traditionalists use. It consists of two boxes - a food box and fire box. The fire box is usually underneath the food box or right next to it, and can be controlled. The smoke and heat from the firebox vents into the food box, and cooks the meat. The most basic versions will use an electric heating element and pan of wood chips, though if you are willing to pay more, advanced smoke boxes let you control the temperature more precisely. The most essential element of smoke boxes is insulation - if you have bad insulation, you won't get good barbeque.

Propane

Propane smokers generate heat using a gas burner that is built underneath a steel (or iron) box that holds wood or charcoal. This steel box has vent holes on top, so very little oxygen gets in. This low-oxygen environment creates the smoke. With propane smokers, you only use a little wood.

Upright drum

These cookers are made from steel, and literally resemble upright drums. The drum includes a cooking rack, basket that holds charcoal at the bottom, and a lid with vents that covers the whole cooker. People use various sizes of steel drums; the most popular is the 55-gallon. You control the smoke temperature by manipulating the amount of air that the bottom (and therefore the charcoal) of the drum gets. Upright drum smokers are usually very efficient when it comes to fuel, and the drippings from meat that fall on the coals burn and evaporate, re-infusing the meat with extra flavors.

Vertical water

The vertical water smoker is a variation of the upright drum. It uses wood or charcoal to generate smoke, but instead of just bare coals, there is a water bowl that sits underneath the grates, so drippings are caught. The water creates humidity and allows the pitmaster to control smoke temperatures more precisely. It also prevents flare-ups that can result from hot meat juice hitting fire. People who use vertical water smokers like the flavor that the blend of water vapor and smoke gives the meat.

Offset

The offset smoker is made of two parts - the cooking chamber and firebox. The cooking part is usually long, grated barrel made of metal with a door and smokestack. The firebox has a door on the top or side, and a vent you can adjust. A hole between the firebox and cooking chamber allows smoke and heat to contact the meat. The smoke escapes from the smoke stack. A lot of the cheap offset smokers aren't very good, and need to be modified by having the doors sealed better. The fireboxes are also often unevenly heated. The more expensive ones are better, and very effective.

Trench

This smoker is built into the ground, with the firebox consisting of a narrow trench that you dig down a slope. It should point into the wind. The middle part of the trench gets covered, while the upper end is made into a chimney where you put your rack of meat. The lower end of the trend, which should be upwind, holds a smoky fire that is feed all day and night, until your meat is cooked. This method is very primitive, and isn't used often.

Electric smokers

The newest of the smokers is also the most convenient and easy to use. The heating element is electric, so it's more easier to control the temperature. With no need to fuel a fire, you can get smoke up to 275-degrees. To get the BBQ flavor, electric smokers also have a box for wood pellets, chunks, or pucks, which generate smoke. Because there's no additional charcoal or wood, the flavor is usually less intense than with traditional smokers.

What if I don't have a smoker?

How can you get BBQ flavor without any type of smoker? It's possible, you just need to follow certain steps. Here's what to do if you have a regular grill:

Prepare wood chips

To smoke, you need wood. We'll discuss what kind of wood imparts what flavors a bit later on, but for now, just know that wood chips like Pecan and Applewood generate a lot of smoke. You'll need to prep them by soaking them in water for 4 hours or more. For even more flavor, save some of that soaking liquid to baste your meat.

Make a foil bag

When your wood chips are ready, you want to get a sheet of aluminum foil and put the chips on it. With another sheet, twist into a bag shape. Poke a few holes into the bag, so the smoke can vent out.

Cook meat using indirect heat

Cooking with indirect heat means you want your meat and charcoal to be on opposite sides, or if you're using an electric grill, only turn on the burners that do not have meat on them. Your chip bag will sit on the burners, as if it were a piece of meat. By closing the grill lid, you surround your meat with the smoke the bag produces.

Cook "low and slow"

This means you want a temperature that's between 225-275 °F. That lets you cook the meat for a long time, 4-5 hours, and really get that smoky flavor into your food.

Spices, spices, and more spices

Even if you follow the steps for smoking without a smoker to the letter, the flavor will likely still not be quite up to par. The key is to use spices with naturally-smoky tones, like cumin, smoked paprika, chipotle, and jalapeno.

What about smoking meat in an oven?

If you want to smoke meat in your oven, you need a raised-grill roasting pan, so the meat doesn't sit in its own juices. Line the pan with aluminum foil, and then add a bed of soaked wood chips. The grill rack goes on top. Put your meat on the rack, and tent with foil. You've made your own mini smoker, with the oven generating the heat. Cook for 4-5 hours at the magical 225-275 °F range. Remember, in an oven, you want to baste the meat as often as you can, or the meat dries out quickly.

Essential smoker equipment and accessories

Once you have your smoker, wood, and other fuel, what else do you need to be on your way to making great BBQ? You technically don't need anything else, but there are accessories that make your life a lot easier and safer. Here's a list of the most important gear:

Meat thermometer

Maintaining the right temperature is crucial to good BBQ, so you need a quality meat thermometer. To avoid having to go out and check it every 20 minutes or so, investing in a good wireless one is very convenient. These let you stick one part into the meat, while the temperature is displayed from a monitor you keep with you. You can be up 100-300 feet away. Some even have timers and alarms, so you'll know when the meat hits a certain temperature.

A long pair of meat tongs

To move meat around, you need a good pair of meat tongs. Long ones are the best, because if they're too short, the smoke and heat can burn you.

Bear claws

These are a little like tongs, but have prongs on them, so they resemble claws. They are great for moving meat and shredding pork, beef, and chicken.

Heat-resistant BBQ gloves

Another good way to avoid burning your hands is to get heat-resistant gloves. These let you handle charcoal and turn food, when you don't want to use tongs that might pull the meat apart too soon. There are gloves specifically made for barbecuing, and they cost around $15-30.

A chimney starter

These little metal devices let you start your fire away from the grill. You put in charcoal, paper towels, some oil, and then light the whole thing. After 10-20 minutes or so, pour into your grill. This lets you get a nice, non-chemical fire going.

A good grill brush

Cleaning your smoker is important, and affects the flavor of the foods you cook. You want a good brush that won't leave behind little wires.

Selecting the right wood

Getting the right wood has a big effect on your barbecue's flavor. Certain woods create certain flavors, so it's wise to know the difference. For starters, you only want to use fruit hardwood, or nut woods. Wood from cedar, pine, elm, redwood, fir, spruce, cypress, or sycamore are not good. You also want to be sure the wood is 100% wood, and free from glue and nails.

What about the cut? If you use wood chips, you always want to soak them in water before using them. This way, they don't burn too quickly. You will probably still need to add more chips if you're cooking for a long time. Wood chunks are the most popular for long, slow cooking times. Full logs are best if you're grilling in a pit or with an offset smoker. They produce a lot of smoke, but take a long time to get there.

Here's a list of the woods available for BBQ, and what kinds of flavors they impart:

Hickory

The most widely-available wood, it has a strong flavor that's best with beef and lamb. Because it's bold, it's best to mix it with other woods so the hickory doesn't overpower the meat. Peach, nectarine, and apricot are good alternatives, because they are milder and sweeter.

Apple

The wood from apple trees is light and sweet, which is perfect for pork, fish, and chicken. Pear has a similar flavor, while crabapple is essentially the same as regular apple. As a note, apple wood will turn chicken skin a dark brown.

Alder

The traditional wood for smoking salmon in the northwestern USA, alder is light and sweet. It's also good for pork and poultry.

Cherry

Cherry wood gives basically any type of meat - beef, pork, poultry - a fruity, sweet flavor. Chokecherry is not the same, and actually gives meat a bitter flavor, so be sure to just get regular cherry wood. It goes really well with hickory.

Citrus

Wood from orange and lemon trees is very mild, more mild than apple or cherry, and gives off a moderate amount of smoke. It's good to mix with other stronger woods. Grapefruit is also a good choice, and smokes every kind of meat.

Maple

Similar to birch wood, maple gives meat a sweet flavor. It's an excellent choice for pork and chicken.

Mesquite

A classic strong-flavored wood, mesquite is famous in Texas. It goes with beef, pork, fish, and poultry. It burns very hot and fast, so it's easy to overdo it.

Oak

A hardwood, oak has a strong smoky flavor that doesn't overwhelm meats like beef and lamb. It's a good choice if you're new to smoking.

Pecan

Pecan wood is very mild, like a mellowed-down hickory. It's similar to almond in its nuttiness, and burns at a very cool temperature, which is great for long, slow barbecuing.

Walnut

Walnut is very smoky and has a strong flavor. It's good to mix with other mellower woods. Black walnut is not the same as regular walnut, and imparts bitter flavors, so don't use interchangeably.

SMOKING BEEF, PORK, POULTRY, AND SEAFOOD

Before we start diving into how to best prepare smoked meats, you should know a bit about spice rubs and sauces. Not every spice rub and sauce goes with every meat, so when you familiarize yourself with regional flavor profiles, you'll have a good idea of what will end up pairing together really well.

Must-know spice rubs

Spice rubs create that much-desired crust on barbecued meat. They also bring out the flavors in the meat, while adding heat, spice, and/or sweetness. The easiest dry rub is simply salt and pepper, but regional BBQ styles each have their own recipes. Enjoy experimenting with unfamiliar rubs that are popular in different areas of the country:

Kansas City

These rubs tend to be very sweet and heavy on the brown sugar. Low and slow cooking is essential, or the sugars burn on the meat. Other seasonings in a KC brown-sugar rub include paprika, salt, chili powder, onion powder, and garlic powder.

Carolinas

Perfect for pork, these rubs are less sugary, and use a few key spices like salt, cumin, paprika, chili powder, and black pepper. It's all about balancing sweet, savory, and heat.

Memphis

This region is all about the rub, since traditionally ribs are served without sauce. The dry rubs is also sprinkled on after the ribs have been smoked. The flavor profile is based on paprika,and gets spicy with cayenne, cumin, and chili powder. A little brown sugar and earthy herbs like thyme and oregano balance out the heat.

Texas

Like Memphis, ribs are usually served "dry," which means there's no sauce. At some places, it's considered insulting to ask for sauce. There's a ton of variety in Texas when it comes to BBQ - it's a big state - but rubs are often very simple with a salt-and-pepper base. The other most common seasonings are paprika, ground cumin, and chili powder.

Must-know sauces

Sauces vary from region to region, while some don't care as much and instead favor dry rubs, which you just read about. Both have their place, and a good sauce can truly distinguish a rack of ribs from the competition. Here are the sauces you should know across the United States:

Kansas City

Thick, sweet, and tangy are the flavors of classic KC barbeque sauces. When most people think of BBQ, they think of Kansas City sauce. The sweet heaviness comes from molasses and ketchup, while seasonings like brown sugar, vinegar, and soy sauce blend together. Each barbeque joint in Kansas City likes to create their own twist on the recipe, so you can find sauces that are more peppery or heavier on the vinegar than others.

North Carolina (East versus West)

In eastern North Carolina, whose cuisine was heavily-influenced by African slaves, you can find vinegar-based sauces, as opposed to tomato ones. The tangy, tart apple cider vinegar and spices like cayenne, red pepper, hot sauce, salt, and black pepper combine to make a thinner sauce that soaks into pork as it cooks. In the western part of the state, you can find more tomato-based sauces, which is considered the "modern" standard.

Lexington-Style (Northern Carolina)

Also known as Piedmont or simply "Red sauce," this sauce is popular in the city of Lexington, North Carolina. It consists of a vinegar-based sauce with ketchup mixed in. When ketchup was first released by Heinz, it actually started a big debate about whether or not the condiment should be used in barbecue. Rumor has it has that five German men began serving pork shoulder with the ketchup-sweetened vinegar sauce, because it was similar to a sauce from Bavaria.

South Carolina

While North Carolina has its vinegar and tomato sauces, South Carolina is all about mustard. This can be traced back to German immigrants, who loved to put mustard on their meat. Thinned out with vinegar, the mustard BBQ sauce includes spices like garlic, chipotle, and sweeteners like honey or light brown sugar. The meat of choice for this sauce is usually pork.

Texas-Style

Because Texas isn't big on thick sauces, "Texas-style" refers to a sauce that's more of a glaze. It's made from beef stock, vinegar, Worcestershire, salt, pepper, garlic, and other spices, and slathered on the meat while it's cooking. This makes it more of a basting sauce than anything else.

Alabama white sauce

One of the more unusual BBQ sauces, this one is creamy and thick. It's a dipping sauce, and was created almost 100 years ago by Bob Gibson, a chef from northern Alabama. It's best served with smoky BBQ chicken and pork, and made from mayonnaise, apple cider vinegar, lemon and apple juice, garlic, horseradish, and black pepper.

Beef

To many - especially Texas - beef is the crown jewel of barbecue. It has more collagen than pork because of the genetic makeup of cattle and the age they're typically raised to, and when you cook beef, that collagen turns into gelatin. The combo of fat and gelatin in the beef is magic to pitmasters. It produces juicy, delicious meat.

Beef distinctions

There's a big debate right now among foodies about grass-fed versus grain-fed beef, but there are actually more terms you should know. Here they are:

Grass-fed: Beef that's been raised eating grass has a more mineral-like taste, and might be healthier than grain-fed cattle. Until the 1950's, grass-fed was the standard.

Grain-fed: Also known as corn-fed, most cattle in the USA are fed with corn. They have more fat, which makes them tastier to a lot of people.

Grass or corn finished: When cattle are "finished," this means they are brought to feedlots and gorged before they get slaughtered. Sometimes grass-fed cattle are finished with corn, which consumers want to know about.

Natural beef: The cattle are not given any hormones or antibiotics.

Organic beef: The cattle must adhere to strict rules to be certified "organic," not just the lack of hormones and antibiotics. They must be fed only organic grains or grass, go outside whenever they want, and treated humanely.

Kosher beef: Also known as halal beef, cattle are raised and slaughtered according to Jewish or Muslim law.

Beef grading

Utility/cutter/canner - The lowest grade of beef used in canned soups, chilis, etc. You won't see it sold in stores by itself.

Standard or commercial - Doesn't have any fat marbling. If a piece of beef is not labeled, it's most likely standard/commercial.

Select - This has just 2-4% fat content.

Choice - A good choice for backyard BBQ, this has some marbling, between 4-10%.

Prime - Considered better and more tender than choice, only 3% of all beef is prime and can only be bought for restaurants. This is the highest rating for all types of beef.

Black Angus - Refers to the breed of cattle, and it's hard to know if the beef you buy is actually Black Angus.

Certified Angus - To be certified Angus, beef must meet 10 quality controls and be either in the top tier of USDA Prime or USDA Choice.

Wagyu - Refers to a Japanese breed of cattle, and is considered the best beef in the world. The famous "kobe beef" is a variety of Wagyu. It's very expensive, and lesser meat is often marked dishonestly as kobe.

How to choose beef at the store

When you're at the store, you usually go for the beef that's pink, because it looks freshest. However, Cargill and other food corporations use a sealing method that lets meat stay pink much longer than usual, even when it's no longer fresh. Always look at the sell-by date, and even if the meat is a little brown, the earliest date will be the most fresh.

Another thing you want to watch out for is blade-tenderized meat. Meat suppliers will use a blade tenderizer to cut through fibers and tissues in the meat, but what happens is dangerous food pathogens can get squished down into the meat. These won't die off during cooking, and you can poison yourself.

Smoking beef brisket

The tough, boneless meat on a cow's chest is called the brisket. When you smoke it, you want a water pan to create humidity, which helps tenderize the beef and regulate temperatures. Put the brisket fat-side up on the cooking rack and cover with the lid. The temperature should be brought up to 225 °F. Check the temp every hour or so, but don't open the lid any more than necessary.

When the brisket itself hits around 150 °F, you will encounter what's known as the "the stall." This is when the inner temperature stops going up. You can either just wait or to speed up the process, wrap the brisket in heavy aluminum foil with ½ cup of apple juice.

A good smoked brisket should have an inner temp of 195 °F, but you want to take it off the grill before that because briskets can go up 10-degrees just sitting on a cutting board. If you like to go by feel, if a fork twists easily inside the meat, it's done.

Pork

Pork doesn't have USDA quality grades like beef. This means the appearance of the pork is the most important factor. You want meat that's firm and pink-gray. A little marbling is also good, because that fat will melt and make the pork juicy. Let's focus on spare ribs. You want a rack that's as even as possible on both sides. There will be some difference, but you don't want a drastic thin-thick ratio. To trim the ribs before cooking, cut away loose pieces of meat and fat. The last step is to remove the layer of skin that's on the boney side of the rack. That's the membrane, and it doesn't get tender during cooking.

Smoking spare ribs

Like with beef, you want a smoker that hangs around 225 F. For ribs, six hours is a good amount of time. Smoke is your friend, so you'll definitely be using lots of wood chips or even wood chunks. When you put the ribs on the rack, put them in the middle. You want lots of airflow and smoke that can surround the meat all over.

A popular method for spare ribs is to cook the ribs without foil for three hours, then wrap them in heavy foil for two, and then finish them off with another hour unwrapped. This lets the ribs get a lot of smoky flavor, and then steam in their juices, so the meat is moist and tender. You want to cook pork to 195-200 F. Rest for 10 minutes before eating.

Poultry

Poultry is graded by the USDA, but they're very simple. It's just A, B, and C. B and C are the lowest grades, and usually consist of all chopped and ground meat. When you get them at a grocery store, they're usually not identified by their grade. Grade A is the highest quality, and means the meat doesn't have any bruises, weird colors, feathers, or broken bones. For whole chickens, it also means the skin doesn't have any tears.

Choosing poultry

How a chicken is raised can affect its taste and quality, just like with beef. There's been a lot of concern lately about how birds are treated in factories, so certain terms have been adopted to let the consumer know what they're buying. Here are the code words you'll see:

Factory farms

This means the poultry are packed together, without free space or outdoor time. They're also given antibiotics to get bigger. If a bird isn't labeled at all, it's probably come from a factory.

Free-range

Free-range chickens don't live in cages and have access to a fenced-in outdoor area at all times. They usually live in indoor space with nests and perches. According to the USDA standards, that "outdoor area" might just consist of a peep hole for the bird to stick its head out of, but not its whole body. Different groups (like HFAC Certified Humane) have different standards.

Pasture-raised

These birds only have access to the outside during the day. The reasoning is that it's too dangerous at night. They typically live in a coop that can be moved around, so the pasture is kept in good shape.

Smoking a whole chicken

One of the great benefits of a smoker is you can use it to cook a whole chicken. It's better than anything you'll get at the store, and you use the whole bird, so there's no waste. The first thing you should know is that your smoker will be at a higher temperature than when you're cooking beef or pork. You want it to be between 250 and 275 F.

To prep the chicken, rinse under cold water and trim any skin or fat that's hanging off. With kitchen string, tie the legs together, and then rub with your chosen spices. Put the chicken on the rack and close the lid. A whole chicken takes around 3-4 hours, or until the internal temperature reaches 165 F. Like all meat, chicken continues to look for a little while after you've taken it out of the smoker, so be careful to not overcook it.

Before cutting into the bird, wait 15-20 minutes.

Seafood

Smoking seafood isn't as common for the backyard BBQ, depending on who you are, but it's just as rewarding and delicious. Because fish has very different muscles than land animals, they never get tough. However, they can get dry, because they don't have much collagen. This means you have to be careful about both the temperature you smoke at it, and the length of time.

Seafood grades

There is no universal labeling system for seafood. Depending on what you're getting (salmon, shrimp, lobster, etc), the grades will be different. The best way to gauge quality is to just use your five senses. Is the fish pink and fresh-looking? Does it smell too fishy? When is the sell-by date?

Sustainability terms

Overfishing has caused a big problem for seafood lovers, so we now have seafood raised in farms. This isn't necessarily a bad thing, because it can help maintain the population in the wild, but it is something consumers like to know about. Half of all seafood is farm-raised, while all fish from Alaska is wild-caught. You can usually find labels that will tell you when something is farm-raised or wild-caught. Here are some to look for:

MSC (*Marine Stewardship Council*): This label is a blue fish with a checkmark, and means that the seafood is wild-caught. To get this certification, a fishery has to prove it has effective strategies for sustainability and the health of the fish population.

Organic: Organic and wild-caught do not mean the same thing. Organic refers to farmed fish. However, if the fish is from the USA and says "organic," it doesn't mean much, because the USDA hasn't finalized organic standards for any farmed fish.

Smoking a whole salmon

Salmon is one of the most popular smoked fish, and very delicious. It's a fatty fish, which is great for BBQ. Fatty fish absorb smoke much better than lean ones. With whole fish, you really don't have to do much prepping besides seasoning. You also want to choose a good wood, like fruity apple or cheddar. Let the chips heat in the smoker for 45 minutes before starting the fish.

For the smoker temp, you want it no higher than 220 F. Maintain that for 1 hour and check the fish's inner temp, which should be at 145 F. Test the thickest part of the fish. Like with all meat, let the fish rest for 10 minutes before devouring!

Introduction to Electric Smokers

Traditional smokers get their heat from gas, wood pellets, or charcoal, as well as wood chips that generate flavor-creating smoke. With electric smokers, however, that heat source is a scalding-hot metal rod instead of gas, wood, or charcoal. The wood chips go above this hot rod, get hold and smoldery, and produce smoke.

ADVANTAGES OF GOING ELECTRIC

Why should you consider getting an electric smoker? There are quite a few reasons why people are choosing electric smokers over traditional methods:

They use clean energy

When you use gas or charcoal as your heat source, the fumes generated are "dirty." They are the kind of fumes that contribute to climate change. There are also a lot of housing complexes like townhouses and apartments that won't let you use gas or charcoal. Electric smokers use clean energy, and release significantly fewer contaminants into the air and into your food.

They don't require babysitting

With traditional smokers, you are in charge of regulating the temperature by feeding it fuel. With electric smokers, the heating source is always consistent. All you have to do is set the temp you want and wait. That gives you time to focus on other parts of your meal or spend time with your friends and family while the food cooks. You can even set an electric smoker to cook food overnight or while you're away from the house.

They conserve energy

Electric smokers don't use very much electricity. They have become very efficient, and only use about 800 watts per hour. Very little heat is lost during the cooking process because of the thick steel construction, which also allows for more even cooking. In terms of wood use, you only need 2-4 ounces to get that classic BBQ smokiness.

Good for beginners

If you don't have experience barbecuing, an electric smoker is one of the best ways to get started. You don't have to know a lot about how much wood to use or how to regulate the smoker temperature to produce great food. Electric smokers are also much safer, so you don't have to be scared of it.

They're easy to clean

Because there's no messy charcoal or gas involved, cleaning an electric smoker is easy. There isn't much fuel residue to deal with, and because most electric smokers are made of stainless steel, wiping off surfaces is fast.

DOWNSIDES OF ELECTRIC SMOKERS

Not everything about electric smokers is all good, and it's important to know what disadvantages you might encounter should you choose one. Here are the three major cons that people bring up:

High prices

Electric smokers tend to be more expensive than traditional ones, because there are more features that have to be built in. There are cheap ones, but those tend to break down quickly, and don't offer the kind of temperature control you need for really good BBQ. There are other things you need in addition to the smoker, as well, like an extension cord that prevents the electric box from overheating.

Lack of the coveted "smoke ring"

The "smoke ring" is a pink layer of meat on the edges of food like brisket and ribs that is part of traditional southern BBQ. This is a result of a chemical reaction between the meat and smoke. Nitrogen dioxide from the wood smoke mixes with the moisture of the meat, creating a layer of nitric acid that produces that pink ring. While it doesn't add flavor, it's the #1 way to tell if a meat has been barbecued properly and authentically. This matters more to some people than others, so it's worth noting that electric smokers don't produce that ring.

Doesn't produce as much as flavor

The biggest downside to electric smokers is that lots of people say the flavor just isn't the same. Because the electrical heating element doesn't add its unique flavor like gas or charcoal does, the meat is often lacking that extra punch. Some people even report that their meat gets a weird flavor from an electric smoker. On the other hand, many are able to get really good food out of an electric smoker, and they are very popular, so clearly something is going right.

Choosing an electric smoker

There are a lot of options when it comes to electric smokers, so how do you choose? What sets one apart from another? Temperature control seems to be a big factor - not all electric smokers let you control the temperature precisely, and not all smokers let you "cold-smoke" food, which is when smoke food without exposing it to heat. It's a popular method for salmon. Generally, the cheaper an electric smoker is, the less control you get over the temperature.

Here are the factors you should think about when choosing an ES:

Temperature control

We really can't overemphasize how crucial this is for good BBQ. Cheaper smokers will use a rheostat. This is basically like a burner on an electric stove that lets you pick low, medium, or high. However, you can't choose precise temperatures. The higher-quality ones will have a thermostat with an attached probe, so you can choose a specific temp and cook the food at that temp. You get both better control over the heat and more precise timing.

The heat flow system

When companies are designing their electric smokers, they choose between an up-to-down heat flow system or down-to-up. Going up-to-down is faster, and more commonly-used by BBQ pros who know what they're doing, while down-to-up cooks the food slower. This ensures better flavor retention for beginners.

Structure of the food tray

Smokers will either have horizontal trays with no inclination, or horizontal trays that do have inclination. Red meat, pork, and poultry tend to cook better on trays that don't incline, while fish likes to cook with inclination. Your choice depends on what you're planning on cooking more often. You should also make the construction of the tray is high-quality, like stainless steel, or something else that's very durable and easy to clean.

Cost vs. value

The last (but not least) factor you should consider as a buyer is how much the smoker costs, and what value you're getting. Does it have all the features you want? Will it last a long time? Will it produce the quality of food you're looking for? Make a list of the most important features and what features you would be okay with giving up. Set a budget. These steps will help you choose an ES that's affordable but definitely worth it.

MOST POPULAR ELECTRIC SMOKER BRANDS

Masterbuilt Electric Smoker (30-inch)

Masterbuilt is one of the most popular brands for electric smokers, and it's not hard to see why. You get 730-square inches of cooking space, complete with an 800-watt heating element and 4 chrome-coated cooking racks. That's enough for 24 hamburgers or 6 whole chickens. You also get easy temperature control with a digital panel and remote, so you just set the temperature and time, and walk away. You can cook between 100-275 F. To load in wood chips, there's a side-loading wood tray.

There's another 30-inch Masterbuilt with a window, so you can see the meat cooking. The thermostat and controls are positioned right on top, and there's a built-in meat probe.

The only real downside people report with this ES is the price. At $300+, it isn't cheap. If you think you wouldn't use the space, it's probably not worth it. If you are serious about getting into BBQ, however, you are paying for consistency-superior results, and that's worth it to a lot of BBQ-lovers.

There are other models of Masterbuilt that are very popular, some more affordable, though those will use analog controls instead of digital. The most budget-friendly Masterbuilt is probably the Portable Electric smoker. It has enough room for a whole turkey, and is small enough to take on camping trips. It has analog temperature controls: off, low, medium, and high.

Smokin - It Model 2

With a stainless-steel construction and capacity for 21 pounds of meat, this electric smoker is a beast. It has enough room for 4 shelves, and comes with 3, which are removable for easier cleaning. Despite its size, it's not hard to move around, and it comes already assembled. To keep the smoker insulated, it has fiberglass. The description says it has a rheostat, but according to the picture on Amazon, you can adjust to specific temperatures between 100-250 F, so it's really a thermostat.

Speaking of the thermostat, some people don't like that that it's built low and close to the burner. This means it runs 7 degrees or so lower than what the top cooking rack actually is. Adjusting the temp could be tricky if you're a beginner.

Char-Broil Vertical Electric Smoker

One of the smaller electric smokers at 505-square feet, it's also more affordable at around $200 or less. The smoking chamber fits three adjustable chrome-coated cooking racks, while the interior is insulated with double walls, so it maintains even temperatures. The heating element has an impressive 1,500 watts and adjustable thermostat for precise cooking. Other pros include a water and wood chip pan and ash pan made from porcelain, so cleaning is easy.

On the downsides, users report being frustrated with the magnetic strips used to keep the door shut. They don't work very well, which is a problem when you need to keep all that heat insulated. They also don't like that the smoker chip box doesn't have a handle.

Bradley Digital 4-Rack Smoker

With a total of 520-square feet of cooking space, you can cook a lot of food in this smoker. This ES also has a higher temperature than other smokers at 280 F. There are also two separate burners, one for generating oven heat, and the other for heating bisquettes (smoker chips) to generate smoke. The most unique feature is the Digital Smoke Generator and automatic advance technology. You set the oven temperature, oven timer, and smoke timer. The tech automatically feeds bisquettes into the burner every 20 minutes, so you get consistent smoke for up to 8 hours.

The most common complaint appears to be that the temperature readings are off 10-15 degrees. This isn't too unusual with electric smokers, so you just have to get used to what your smoker does and adjust accordingly.

Pork Recipes

Contents

Smoked Barbecue Pork Belly 34

Smoked Pork Chops... 35

Barbecue Pork Shoulder 36

Smoked Pork Tenderloin 37

Smoked Ribs with Chipotle and Lime 38

Smoked Andouille Sausage.................................... 39

Smoked Ham and Cheese Fatty 40

Smoked Italian Sausage... 41

Smoked Kielbasa 42

Smoked Barbecue Ribs 43

Smoked Salsa Fatty Meatloaf 44

Homemade Bacon.. 45

Honey Glazed Smoked Ham................................... 46

Smoked Pulled Pork 47

Smoked Pork Butt 48

Perfect Smoked Pork.. 49

Smoked Barbecue Pork Belly

Serves: 8 / Preparation time: 5 minutes / Cooking time: 8 hours

This is a classic slow-cooked barbecue oozing with juice and sauce. For this recipe, it is recommended to use skinless pork belly. This will let the smoke and flavor seep into the meat well.

4 pounds unseasoned pork belly, cut thick

2 cups apple juice

½ cup barbecue sauce

¼ cup sweet rub

For the sweet rub:

¼ cup dark brown sugar

1 tablespoon rock sea salt

2 teaspoons cracked black pepper

2 teaspoons garlic powder

2 teaspoons onion powder

2 teaspoons smoked paprika

1 teaspoon ground mustard

½ teaspoon cayenne pepper

- Mix all sweet rub ingredients in a bowl. Stir well and keep in a sealed container.
- Preheat smoker to 225 F.
- Mark the top layer of pork belly fat in 1-inch squares with a sharp knife. Season generously with the sweet rub on both sides.
- Put the cured pork belly on the smoker. Smoke for about 6 hours or until temperature reaches 165 F. Spray with apple juice every hour while cooking.
- Remove pork belly from the smoker.
- Wrap in aluminum foil with ½ cup apple juice. Fully seal the ends of the foil and put back on the smoker until temperature reaches 200 F.
- Unwrap pork belly and sprinkle with the apple juice from the foil. Put back the pork belly on the smoker and glaze with barbecue sauce. Cook for 10 minutes.
- Remove pork belly from the smoker. Let it cool for 15 minutes. Chop into cubes.

Per Serving: Calories: 374; Total Fat: 30g; Saturated Fat: 11g; Protein: 22g; Carbs: 4g; Fiber: 1g; Sugar: 2g

Smoked Pork Chops

Serves: 4 / Preparation time: 5 minutes / Cooking time: 1 hour 55 minutes

This recipe can be used by beginner smokers. Having the right meat is the first step to a perfect smoked pork chop. Ask the butcher to cut the meat thick for this recipe.

4 pork chops, cut thick

1 ½ tablespoons salt

1 tablespoon black pepper

1 tablespoon onion powder

1 tablespoon smoked paprika

½ tablespoon garlic powder

Olive oil

- Preheat smoker to 250 F.
- Mix salt, black pepper, onion powder, smoked paprika and garlic powder in a bowl.
- Glaze pork chops with olive oil and then season with mixture on both sides.
- Put grill on high heat. Sear pork chops on each side until slight crust is formed.
- Put seared pork chops on the smoker.   Smoke for about 1 hour and 30 minutes or until temperature reaches 145 F.
- Remove pork chops from the smoker. Let it cool for 10 minutes.

Per Serving: Calories: 321; Total Fat: 15g; Saturated Fat: 5g; Protein: 39g; Carbs: 0g; Fiber: 1g; Sugar: 0g

Barbecue Pork Shoulder

Serves: 16 / Preparation time: 10 minutes / Cooking time: 14 hours

This recipe calls for a whole day at home, but you can still do other tasks while cooking. The neighbors will wonder what's cooking because of its delicious smell that fills the air for hours.

8 pounds pork shoulder

¾ cup barbecue rub

3 chunks medium smoking oak or hickory wood

For the braise:

¾ cup apple juice

¼ cup barbecue sauce

¼ cup brown sugar

¼ cup cider vinegar

2 tablespoons agave syrup

2 tablespoons jalapeño jelly

2 tablespoons Worcestershire sauce

For the injection:

½ cup apple juice

¼ cup brown sugar

3 tablespoons cider vinegar

3 tablespoons water

2 tablespoons Kosher salt

2 tablespoons Worcestershire sauce

- Mix all the braise ingredients in a bowl. Stir well and set aside.
- Mix all the injection ingredients in a bowl, then inject pork at 1-inch intervals using an injection syringe and pat dry using paper towels.
- Season generously with the barbecue rub on both sides.
- Heat smoker to 225 F. Add chunks of wood.
- Once smoke is produced, put pork shoulder on the smoker. Smoke for about 7 hours or until color turned to deep mahogany.
- Remove pork shoulder from the smoker.
- Wrap in aluminum foil with 1 cup of braise. Fully seal the ends of the foil and put back on the smoker until temperature reaches 198 F.
- Remove pork shoulder from the smoker and unwrap. Let it cool for 30 minutes.
- Pull pork shoulder into chunks and put in a medium pan. Pour remaining braise and mix. Serve immediately.

Per Serving: Calories: 303; Total Fat: 15g; Saturated Fat: 5g; Protein: 29g; Carbs: 8g; Fiber: 0g; Sugar: 6g

Smoked Pork Tenderloin

Serves: 2 / Preparation time: 5 minutes / Cooking time: 3 hours

Pork tenderloin as the name goes is incredibly tender. It is very lean but sometimes there are some chunks of fat. You can trim that excess fat easily if you prefer.

1 pork tenderloin   3 tablespoons rub of choice

¼ cup barbecue sauce

- Preheat smoker to 225 F.
- Remove fat or silver skin from tenderloin.
- Season generously with the rub on all sides.
- Put pork tenderloin on the smoker. Smoke for about 3 hours or until temperature reaches 145 F.
- Glaze the pork with barbecue sauce after 2 ½ hours on the smoker.
- Remove pork tenderloin from the smoker. Let it cool for 10 minutes.

Per Serving: Calories: 350; Total Fat: 17g; Saturated Fat: 7g; Protein: 18g; Carbs: 27g; Fiber: 0g; Sugar: 5g

Smoked Ribs with Chipotle and Lime

Serves: 4 / Preparation time: 20 minutes / Cooking time: 6 hours

This recipe is done with the 3-2-1 method: smoke for 3 hours, bake for 2 hours and grill for 1 hour. You can serve the ribs with additional barbecue sauce, lime wedges and cilantro.

2 racks back ribs

1 cup barbecue rub

2 tablespoons ground cumin

1 cup apple juice

For the chipotle and lime barbecue sauce:

¼ cup butter

1 onion, diced

1 yellow pepper, diced

1 small can chipotle peppers in adobo sauce

1 small can tomato paste

1/3 cup brown sugar

3 tablespoons honey

2 tablespoons molasses

1 ½ teaspoon lime zest

3 limes, juiced

For the chipotle and lime barbecue sauce:

- Melt butter in a saucepan. Fry the onion and pepper.
- Add chipotle peppers, tomato paste, brown sugar, honey, molasses, lime zest and lime juice. Let it boil.
- Lower the heat and let it simmer for 20 minutes.
- Remove from heat and let it cool.
- Blend until smooth.

For the back ribs:

- Remove membrane from back of ribs. Mix barbecue rub with ground cumin.
- Season ribs generously with the rub on all sides. Put in the fridge for 1 hour.
- Preheat smoker to 225 F.
- Smoke back ribs for 3 hours.
- Remove back ribs from the smoker. Put in a roasting pan. Add apple juice. Cover the pan with a lid. Bake in an oven for 2 hours at 225 F.
- Remove back ribs from the oven. Put on the barbecue set at 250 F.
- Glaze with chipotle and lime barbecue sauce. Grill for 1 hour. Be careful not to burn.

Per Serving: Calories: 525; Total Fat: 27g; Saturated Fat: 6g; Protein: 15g; Carbs: 61g; Fiber: 7g; Sugar: 42g

Smoked Andouille Sausage

Serves: 10 / Preparation time: 1 hour / Cooking time: 4 hours

Andouille is a smoked sausage made with pork which originated in France. Andouille is a popular ingredient in many Cajun dishes.

5 pounds pork shoulder or fresh ham

Sausage casings

For the mixture:

1 cup cold water

½ cup skim milk powder

2 tablespoons garlic powder

2 tablespoons dried chili flakes

1 tablespoon paprika

1 tablespoon ground black pepper

1 tablespoon cayenne pepper

4 teaspoons dried thyme

3 teaspoons salt

1 teaspoon cure

- Slice pork meat and fat into 2-inch cubes. Grind 2/3 of pork meat. Dice into small chunks the remaining 1/3 of pork meat.
- Combine the meat with the mixture ingredients. Mix thoroughly. Place in the fridge for 3 hours.
- Fill sausage casings with the meat mixture.
- Preheat smoker to 130 F.
- Put the sausage on the smoker. Smoke for 4 hours.
- Remove sausage from the smoker. Soak in hot water bath at 165 F for 45 minutes.
- Remove sausage from the hot water bath and hang for 2 hours.

Per Serving: Calories: 454; Total Fat: 23g; Saturated Fat: 6g; Protein: 53g; Carbs: 2g; Fiber: 0g; Sugar: 0g

Smoked Ham and Cheese Fatty

Serves: 4 / Preparation time: 20 minutes / Cooking time: 2 hours 30 minutes

A fatty is spiced ground pork that you can stuff with different ingredients. Stuff, roll, smoke and enjoy a fatty.

1 pound ground pork

4 slices ham lunchmeat

½ cup diced onion

½ cup diced pepper

1/3 cup cream cheese

¼ cup barbecue sauce

1 tablespoon barbecue rub

1 tablespoon butter

- Melt butter in a saucepan. Fry the onion and pepper. Let it cool.
- Mix ground pork with barbecue rub, fried onion and pepper.
- Spread mixture in a rectangle pan.
- Put 2 slices of ham at the middle of the meat. Put cream cheese on the ham.
- Use the remaining 2 slices of ham to wrap around the cream cheese.
- Roll up the fatty to enclose the ham and cheese with the pork mixture.
- Preheat smoker to 250 F.
- Put the fatty on the smoker. Smoke for 2 ½ hours or until temperature reaches 165 F.
- Glaze the fatty with barbecue sauce after 1 ½ hours on the smoker.

Per Serving: Calories: 260; Total Fat: 18g; Saturated Fat: 7g; Protein: 15g; Carbs: 13g; Fiber: 0g; Sugar: 5g

Smoked Italian Sausage

Serves: 4 / Preparation time: 5 minutes / Cooking time: 3 hours

Italian sausages are readily available and can be smoked for a couple of hours. You can add smoked Italian sausages to other recipes to enhance taste with a smoky flavor.

2 pounds fresh Italian sausage covered with casing

- Preheat smoker to 250 F.
- Put the Italian sausage on the smoker with spaces of at least ½ inch between.
- Smoke for about 3 hours or until temperature reaches 165 F.

Per Serving: Calories: 239; Total Fat: 19g; Saturated Fat: 8g; Protein: 14g; Carbs: 3g; Fiber: 0g; Sugar: 0g

Smoked Kielbasa

Serves: 4 / Preparation time: 1 hour / Cooking time: 5 hours

Kielbasa is a type of sausage that originated from Poland and Ukraine. Kielbasa is a Polish word meaning sausage.

5 pounds pork shoulder or fresh ham

Sausage casings

For the mixture:

1 cup cold water

½ cup skim milk powder

2 tablespoons garlic powder

3 teaspoons salt

3 teaspoons ground black pepper

2 teaspoons dried marjoram

1 teaspoon cure

- Slice pork meat and fat into 2-inch cubes. Grind 2/3 of pork meat. Dice into small chunks the remaining 1/3 of pork meat.
- Combine the meat with the mixture ingredients. Mix thoroughly. Place in the fridge for 3 hours.
- Fill sausage casings with the meat mixture.
- Preheat smoker to 130 F.
- Put the sausage on the smoker. Smoke for 4 hours.
- Remove sausage from the smoker. Soak in hot water bath at 165 F for 45 minutes.
- Remove sausage from the hot water bath and hang for 2 hours.

Per Serving: Calories: 300; Total Fat: 24g; Saturated Fat: 9g; Protein: 14g; Carbs: 8g; Fiber: 0g; Sugar: 2g

Smoked Barbecue Ribs

Serves: 6 / Preparation time: 25 minutes / Cooking time: 5 hours

One of the secrets in cooking smoked barbecue ribs is perfecting time and temperature. You can use the thermometer on the smoker or use an oven thermometer and place it on the rack.

2 racks St. Louis ribs

1 bottle barbecue sauce

1 cup apple juice

¾ cup barbecue rub

- Remove membrane from back of ribs.
- Season ribs generously with the rub on all sides. Set aside for 20 minutes.
- Preheat smoker to 225 F.
- Smoke for about 4 ½ hours or until temperature reaches 201 F.
- Spray the ribs with apple juice after 1 hour on the smoker. Spray every after 45 minutes.
- Glaze with barbecue sauce thinly on both sides. Let sit for 10 minutes.
- Remove ribs from the smoker. Let it cool for 10 minutes.
- Slice and serve with barbecue sauce.

Per Serving: Calories: 661; Total Fat: 42g; Saturated Fat: 13g; Protein: 28g; Carbs: 49g; Fiber: 3g; Sugar: 43g

Smoked Salsa Fatty Meatloaf

Serves: 4 / Preparation time: 15 minutes / Cooking time: 2 hours 30 minutes

This is a simple recipe that you can do in a short amount of time and without much effort but the result is a super tasty meal. It's just salsa and cheese stuffed in rolled-up ground pork.

1 ½ pounds ground pork

1 cup salsa

1 ½ cups cheddar cheese, grated

For the mixture:

1 teaspoon chili powder

½ teaspoon dried oregano

½ teaspoon garlic powder

½ teaspoon salt

- Combine meat with the mixture ingredients. Mix thoroughly.
- Spread mixture in a square pan.
- Put salsa at the middle of the meat. Sprinkle with grated cheese.
- Roll up the fatty to enclose the cheese and salsa with the pork mixture.
- Preheat smoker to 250 F.
- Put the fatty on the smoker. Smoke for 2 ½ hours or until temperature reaches 165 F.

Per Serving: Calories: 343; Total Fat: 26g; Saturated Fat: 10g; Protein: 17g; Carbs: 10g; Fiber: 1g; Sugar: 2g

Homemade Bacon

Serves: 10 / Preparation time: 30 minutes / Cooking time: 3 hours

Bacon is easily available in stores but making your own bacon can be tastier, slightly healthier and cheaper than store-bought bacon. Making your own bacon is fun yet challenging, but in the end, it's satisfying to know that you can make it on your own and even better than what they sell at the store.

5 pounds pork belly, with skin

For the spice rub:

¼ cup dark brown sugar

¼ cup honey

¼ cup kosher salt

2 tablespoons red pepper flakes

2 tablespoons smoked sweet paprika

2 teaspoons pink curing salt

1 teaspoon cumin seeds

- Mix all the spice rub ingredients in a bowl. Stir well and keep in a sealed container.
- Season belly generously with the rub on all sides.
- Put in a plastic bag. Put in the fridge for 7 days. Flip everyday until firm.
- Remove from the bag, rinse and dry belly. Put in the fridge for 2 days.
- Preheat smoker to 200 F.
- Put the belly on the smoker. Smoke for 3 hours or until temperature reaches 150 F.
- Remove from smoker. Slice and cook.
- Wrap bacon in a plastic wrap to store. Can be placed in a fridge for 1 week or in a freezer for 2 months.

Per Serving: Calories: 200; Total Fat: 14g; Saturated Fat: 6g; Protein: 10g; Carbs: 17g; Fiber: 0g; Sugar: 12g

Honey Glazed Smoked Ham

Serves: 12 / Preparation time: 30 minutes / Cooking time: 6 hours

This is a way of turning an ordinary ready to eat ham into something extraordinary. It may take longer to prepare but it tastes better.

6 pounds ready to eat ham

For the rub:

1 tablespoon black pepper

1 tablespoon paprika

1 tablespoon sugar

1 teaspoon dry mustard

2 teaspoons salt

½ teaspoon cayenne

For the sauce:

¾ cups chicken stock

¾ cups pineapple juice

2 tablespoons vegetable oil

½ teaspoon dry mustard

½ teaspoon ground cloves

For the glaze:

½ cup honey

¼ cup pineapple juice

½ teaspoon dry mustard

Pinch of ground cloves

- Combine the rub ingredients. Mix thoroughly.
- Season ham generously with the rub mixture. Wrap in foil. Put in the fridge overnight.
- The next day, remove ham from the fridge. Let it sit for 1 hour and unwrap.
- Preheat smoker to 210 F.
- Combine the sauce ingredients. Mix thoroughly. Warm over medium heat.
- Put the seasoned ham on the smoker. Smoke for 6 hours.
- Season with sauce every hour.
- Combine the glaze ingredients. Mix thoroughly.
- Glaze ham after 5 hours on the smoker.

Per Serving: Calories: 215; Total Fat: 7g; Saturated Fat: 2g; Protein: 19g; Carbs: 20g; Fiber: 0g; Sugar: 20g

Smoked Pulled Pork

Serves: 20 / Preparation time: 10 minutes / Cooking time: 8 hours

Pulled pork is a method of cooking where meat is cooked slowly allowing the meat to become tender and easily pulled. Before cooking, meat is soaked in brine to provide the moisture needed for the slow cooking process.

8 pounds pork shoulder roast

1 quart apple cider

1 onion, chopped

For the rub:

5 tablespoons light brown sugar

5 tablespoons white sugar

2 tablespoons kosher salt

2 tablespoons paprika

1 tablespoon freshly ground black pepper

1 tablespoon garlic powder

1 tablespoon onion powder

- Put pork shoulder in a large pot. Add apple cider to soak.
- Combine the rub ingredients. Mix thoroughly.
- Put ¼ cup rub mixture to the pork shoulder.
- Cover pot. Put in the fridge for 12 hours.
- Preheat smoker to 210 F.
- Put cider marinade into the smoker water pan. Add onion and ¼ cup rub mixture.
- Season pork shoulder with the remaining rub. Put pork shoulder on the smoker.
- Smoke for 8 hours or until very tender.
- Remove pork shoulder from smoker. Let it cool for 30 minutes.
- Shred with fork.

Per Serving: Calories: 240; Total Fat: 6g; Saturated Fat: 3g; Protein: 26g; Carbs: 12g; Fiber: 1g; Sugar: 10g

Smoked Pork Butt

Serves: 16 / Preparation time: 20 minutes / Cooking time: 18 hours

Having a delicious smoked pork butt calls for fresh meat. Look for a pork butt that has large money muscle and horn muscle.

7 pounds fresh pork butt roast

2 tablespoons chili powder

4 tablespoons brown sugar

- Soak pork butt in brine solution. Cover and put in the fridge overnight.
- Preheat smoker to 225 F.
- Combine brown sugar and chili powder. Mix thoroughly.
- Season meat with the mixture generously.
- Put the seasoned meat on the smoker. Smoke for 18 hours or until temperature reaches 145 F.

Per Serving: Calories: 326; Total Fat: 15g; Saturated Fat: 5g; Protein: 29g; Carbs: 8g; Fiber: 0g; Sugar: 6g

Perfect Smoked Pork

Serves: 8 / Preparation time: 15 minutes / Cooking time: 6 hours

Perfect smoked pork is wonderfully moist and tender. A recipe with herbs and no salt, perfect for folks who are watching their salt intake.

8 pounds fresh ham

For the rub:

½ cup olive oil

¼ cup parsley, chopped

4 tablespoons light brown sugar ·

½ teaspoon fresh oregano

½ teaspoon fresh thyme

8 large fresh basil leaves

6 garlic cloves

- Combine all rub ingredients except sugar. Blend until thick.
- Season ham with the mixture generously. Sprinkle with sugar. Wrap in a foil.
- Place in the fridge overnight.
- Preheat smoker to 275 F.
- Unwrap the ham. Put on the smoker.
- Smoke for about 6 hours or until temperature reaches 170 F.
- Remove ham from the smoker. Let it cool for 20 minutes.
- Serve with barbecue sauce.

Per Serving: Calories: 560; Total Fat: 20g; Saturated Fat: 8g; Protein: 80g; Carbs: 8g; Fiber: 0g; Sugar: 8g

Beef Recipes

Contents

Barbecue Smoked Beef Chuck 52

Texas Style Smoked Beef Brisket 53

Smoked Beef Ribs... 54

Smoked Beef Stew 55

Smoked Beef Jerky 56

Smoked Roast Beef 57

Smoked Beef Burnt Ends 58

Smoked Beef Tenderloin 59

Grass-Fed Beef Sirloin Kebabs 60

Smoky Caramelized Onion Burgers 61

Smoked Pulled Beef 62

Barbecue Beef Sandwich 63

Smoked Beef Rump Roast 64

Montreal Smoked Meat 65

Barbecue Smoked Beef Chuck

Serves: 10 / Preparation time: 10 minutes / Cooking time: 10 hours

Beef chuck is cheaper than brisket but still turns out tender and tasty when smoked low and slow. This recipe calls for just salt and pepper rub.

5 pounds beef chuck roll   ¼ cup kosher salt

1/3 cup ground black peppercorn

- Combine pepper and salt.
- Season beef with the mixture generously.
- Preheat smoker to 275 F.
- Put beef on the smoker. Smoke for about 4 hours or until temperature reaches 165 F.
- Remove beef from the smoker. Wrap in aluminum foil.
- Put beef back on the smoker. Smoke for about 5 hours or until temperature reaches 140 F.
- Remove beef from the smoker. Let it cool for 30 minutes.
- Slice meat thinly.
- Serve with onion, pickles and white bread.

Per Serving: Calories: 422; Total Fat: 24g; Saturated Fat: 10g; Protein: 47g; Carbs: 0g; Fiber: 0g; Sugar: 0g

Texas Style Smoked Beef Brisket

Serves: 20 / Preparation time: 30 minutes / Cooking time: 18 hours

Brisket is coming from the cow's breast or lower chest. It is rich in connective tissue that requires a slow process to soften the muscle.

14 pounds whole brisket

2 tablespoons garlic powder

2 tablespoons ground black pepper

2 tablespoons kosher salt

- Remove fat or silver skin from brisket.
- Combine garlic powder, pepper and salt.
- Season beef with the mixture generously.
- Preheat smoker to 225 F.
- Put beef on the smoker. Smoke for about 8 hours or until temperature reaches 165 F.
- Remove beef from the smoker. Wrap in aluminum foil.
- Put beef back on the smoker. Smoke for about 8 hours or until temperature reaches 200 F.
- Remove beef from the smoker. Let it cool for 1 hour.
- Slice meat and serve.

Per Serving: Calories: 250; Total Fat: 19g; Saturated Fat: 7g; Protein: 18g; Carbs: 1g; Fiber: 0g; Sugar: 0g

Smoked Beef Ribs

Serves: 1 rack / Preparation time: 10 minutes / Cooking time: 3 hours

Pork ribs are more popular than beef ribs, and that's probably why beef ribs are usually cheaper. Low and slow is the key to smoking beef ribs perfectly.

1 rack beef ribs

1 cup barbecue sauce

For the rub:

2 tablespoons paprika

2 tablespoons sugar

1 tablespoon chili powder

1 tablespoon garlic powder

1 tablespoon salt

1 ½ teaspoon dry mustard

1 teaspoon black pepper

1 teaspoon cumin

1 teaspoon oregano

½ teaspoon cayenne pepper

- Combine rub ingredients. Mix thoroughly.
- Remove membrane from brisket.
- Season beef with the mixture generously. Put in the fridge for 3 hours.
- Preheat smoker to 225 F.
- Put beef on the smoker. Smoke for 3 hours.
- Remove beef from the smoker. Glaze with barbecue sauce.
- Remove beef from the smoker. Let it cool for 10 minutes.
- Slice meat and serve.

Per Serving: Calories: 1,058; Total Fat: 89g; Saturated Fat: 37g; Protein: 60g; Carbs: 41g; Fiber: 0g; Sugar: 20g

Smoked Beef Stew

Serves: 8 / Preparation time: 30 minutes / Cooking time: 10 hours

Smoking is often done during summer. During the cold winter days, you can still use your smoker to cook up a nice smoked beef stew.

2 pounds stewing beef, cubed

5 cups beef broth

1 can diced tomatoes

8 carrots, peeled and diced

8 medium potatoes, peeled and diced

2 onions, diced

2 tablespoons corn starch

2 tablespoons water

For the rub:

1 tablespoon paprika

1 tablespoon sugar

2 teaspoon dry oregano

1 teaspoon garlic powder

1 teaspoon ground black pepper

1 teaspoon salt

½ teaspoon cayenne pepper

½ teaspoon thyme

- Combine rub ingredients. Mix thoroughly.
- Season beef with the mixture generously.
- Preheat smoker to 225 F.
- Put beef on the smoker. Smoke for about 2 hours.
- Remove beef from the smoker. Put in a slow cooker.
- Add beef broth, tomatoes, carrots, potatoes and onions.
- Cook for 8 hours on low heat.
- Whip corn starch and water together. Add to the slow cooker 15 minutes before finishing the stew.
- Serve with fresh bread.

Per Serving: Calories: 386; Total Fat: 18g; Saturated Fat: 6g; Protein: 52g; Carbs: 28g; Fiber: 4g; Sugar: 2g

Smoked Beef Jerky

Serves: 6 / Preparation time: 10 minutes / Cooking time: 7 hours

Jerky is long thin strips of meat that have been dried. Typically, beef is used in making jerky and the traditional method is drying in the sun.

2 pounds sirloin, sliced ½ inch thick

1 cup soy sauce

4 tablespoons ground black pepper

1 tablespoon cider vinegar

1 dash hot pepper sauce

1 dash Worcestershire sauce

- Combine all ingredients in a bowl except for the beef. Mix well.
- Add beef slices. Cover and place in the fridge overnight.
- Preheat smoker to 170 F.
- Put beef on the smoker. Smoke for about 7 hours or until jerky edges appear dry.

Per Serving: Calories: 220; Total Fat: 4g; Saturated Fat: 2g; Protein: 28g; Carbs: 6g; Fiber: 0g; Sugar: 3g

Smoked Roast Beef

Serves: 8 / Preparation time: 20 minutes / Cooking time: 5 hours

Smoked roast beef can be eaten as a main dish or can be made into roast beef sandwich. It goes great with mashed potatoes and macaroni & cheese.

3 pounds beef rump roast

For the rub:

1 ½ teaspoon salt

1 teaspoon garlic powder

1 teaspoon pepper

1 teaspoon smoked paprika

½ teaspoon onion powder

Worcestershire sauce

- Combine all ingredients except for the Worcestershire sauce. Mix well.
- Rub beef with Worcestershire sauce. Season with the mixture.
- Preheat smoker to 200 F.
- Put beef on the smoker. Smoke for about 5 hours or until temperature reaches 150 F.
- Remove beef from the smoker. Let it cool for 20 minutes.
- Slice and serve.

Per Serving: Calories: 298; Total Fat: 10g; Saturated Fat: 4g; Protein: 46g; Carbs: 19g; Fiber: 0g; Sugar: 10g

Smoked Beef Burnt Ends

Serves: 6 / Preparation time: 15 minutes / Cooking time: 10 hours

This recipe is loaded with fatty marbling and amazing flavor. Serve with white bread, pickles and onions.

3 pounds chuck roast

½ cup barbecue sauce

¼ cup brown sugar

2 tablespoons brown sugar

For the rub:

1 tablespoon garlic powder

1 tablespoon ground black pepper

1 tablespoon kosher salt

- Preheat smoker to 275 F.
- Combine rub ingredients.
- Season beef generously with the rub mixture.
- Put beef on the smoker. Smoke for about 5 hours or until temperature reaches 165 F.
- Remove beef from the smoker. Wrap in aluminum foil.
- Put beef back on the smoker. Smoke for about 1 hour or until temperature reaches 195 F.
- Remove beef from the smoker. Let it cool for 20 minutes.
- Slice and transfer to a foil pan.
- Sprinkle with ¼ cup sugar and drizzle with barbecue sauce.
- Put pan on the smoker, close lid and cook for 2 hours.
- Sprinkle with 2 tablespoons sugar and drizzle with barbecue sauce.
- Stir and grill for a few minutes.

Per Serving: Calories: 208; Total Fat: 5g; Saturated Fat: 2g; Protein: 30g; Carbs: 11g; Fiber: 0g; Sugar: 11g

Smoked Beef Tenderloin

Serves: 8 / Preparation time: 25 minutes / Cooking time: 1 hour

Since beef tenderloin is pricey, you can substitute it with budget-friendly steaks. Serve with mustard cream sauce or horseradish cream sauce.

4 pounds beef tenderloin

2 tablespoons extra virgin olive oil

Kosher salt

Ground black pepper

- Preheat smoker to 300 F.
- Season beef generously with salt and pepper. Drizzle with olive oil and then put beef on the smoker for about 45 minutes or until temperature reaches 125 F.
- Remove beef from the smoker. Let it cool for 10 minutes.
- Slice thinly and serve.

Per Serving: Calories: 483; Total Fat: 18g; Saturated Fat: 8g; Protein: 75g; Carbs: 0g; Fiber: 0g; Sugar: 0g

Grass-Fed Beef Sirloin Kebabs

Serves: 4 / Preparation time: 25 minutes / Cooking time: 3 minutes

If you can't find top sirloin, you can substitute it with bottom round or strip steaks. You can also prepare the sauce and skewer the beef ahead of time.

1 pound grass-fed top sirloin steak, trimmed

8 skewers

Cooking spray

2 tablespoons olive oil

1 teaspoon ground coriander

1 teaspoon black pepper

¾ teaspoon kosher salt

For the sauce:

½ cup plain 2% reduced-fat Greek yogurt

2 tablespoons fresh dill, chopped

1 tablespoon fresh lemon juice

1 tablespoon lemon rind, grated

¼ teaspoon kosher salt

- Preheat smoker to 550 F.
- Combine sauce ingredients. Mix thoroughly.
- Cut steak into 16 strips. Mix with oil, coriander, pepper and salt.
- Thread 2 steak strips into each skewer.
- Put skewers on the smoker coated with cooking spray. Smoke for about 90 seconds on each side.
- Serve with yogurt sauce.

Per Serving: Calories: 244; Total Fat: 14g; Saturated Fat: 6g; Protein: 27g; Carbs: 4g; Fiber: 0g; Sugar: 3g

Smoky Caramelized Onion Burgers

Serves: 4 / Preparation time: 25 minutes / Cooking time: 20 minutes

This recipe turns an ordinary grilled beef patty into something extraordinary. With caramelized onions and garlic, the burgers are kept moist.

For the patties:

1 pound 90% lean ground sirloin

1 ½ cups yellow onion, thinly sliced

1 ½ tablespoons minced garlic

½ tablespoon ground cumin

½ tablespoon olive oil

1 teaspoon smoked paprika

1 teaspoon kosher salt

1 teaspoon ground black pepper

Cooking spray

For the burgers:

4 whole-wheat hamburger buns

4 tomato slices

2 red onion slices

1 cup baby arugula leaves

2 tablespoons canola mayonnaise

2 tablespoons roasted red bell pepper, finely chopped

1 tablespoon minced fresh chives

- Preheat smoker to 450 F.
- In a skillet, put oil over medium heat. Sauté yellow onion until golden brown.
- Add garlic, cook until fragrant.
- Remove skillet from heat. Let cool. Put onion mixture in a large bowl.
- Add the rest of patty ingredients. Mix thoroughly.
- Shape beef mixture into 4 patties.
- Coat smoker with cooking spray. Put patties on the smoker. Smoke for 4 minutes on each side.
- Remove patties from the smoker.
- In a bowl, mix bell pepper, mayonnaise and chives. Mix thoroughly.
- Put patties on bottom halves of buns. Layer with tomato, red onion, arugula, mayonnaise mixture and top halves of buns.

Per Serving: Calories: 340; Total Fat: 26g; Saturated Fat: 10g; Protein: 23g; Carbs: 29g; Fiber: 1g; Sugar: 5g

Smoked Pulled Beef

Serves: 10 / Preparation time: 10 minutes / Cooking time: 12 hours

Pulled pork has been popular, but pulled beef has all the good qualities of pulled pork and some folks prefer the taste. Chuck roast is the best meat to use for the pulled beef.

6 pounds chuck roast

3 cups beef stock

1 yellow onion, sliced

For the rub:

2 tablespoons black pepper

2 tablespoons garlic powder

2 tablespoons kosher salt

- Preheat smoker to 225 F.
- Combine the rub ingredients. Mix thoroughly.
- Season beef roast generously with the rub mixture.
- Put beef on the smoker. Smoke for about 3 hours.
- Spray with 1 cup of beef stock every hour while smoking.
- Spread sliced onions in an aluminum pan. Pour 2 cups of beef stock. Place the beef roast on top of the onions.
- Put the pan on the smoker. Increase temperature to 250 F.
- Smoke for about 3 hours or until temperature reaches 165 F.
- Cover the pan tightly with aluminum foil. Continue smoking for 5 hours or until temperature reaches 202 F.

Per Serving: Calories: 422; Total Fat: 24g; Saturated Fat: 10g; Protein: 47g; Carbs: 0g; Fiber: 0g; Sugar: 0g

Barbecue Beef Sandwich

Serves: 14 / Preparation time: 15 minutes / Cooking time: 5 hours

Barbecue Beef Sandwich is something tasty to put in your brown lunch bag. You can prepare the beef during the weekend and easily pull out a sandwich during the weekdays.

3 pounds beef chuck roast

14 sesame seed hamburger buns, split

For the rub:

1 medium onion, chopped

2 garlic cloves, minced

2 cups ketchup

¼ cup cider vinegar

¼ cup molasses

2 tablespoons Worcestershire sauce

½ teaspoon ground mustard

½ teaspoon pepper

½ teaspoon salt

¼ teaspoon garlic powder

¼ teaspoon red pepper flakes, crushed

- Preheat smoker to 250 F.
- Combine rub ingredients. Mix thoroughly.
- Season beef generously with the rub mixture.
- Put beef on the smoker. Smoke for about 3 ½ hours or until temperature reaches 160 F.
- Remove beef from the smoker. Wrap in aluminum foil.
- Put beef back on the smoker. Smoke for about 1 ½ hours or until temperature reaches 204 F.
- Remove beef from the smoker. Shred meat.
- Serve beef on buns.

Per Serving: Calories: 325; Total Fat: 15g; Saturated Fat: 5g; Protein: 30g; Carbs: 29g; Fiber: 1g; Sugar: 5g

Smoked Beef Rump Roast

Serves: 8 / Preparation time: 15 minutes / Cooking time: 3 ½ hours

When smoking a rump roast, cooking takes care of itself. Just rub the meat, then let the heat and smoke take care of the rest.

3 pounds Angus beef rump roast

2 cups beef broth

Yellow mustard

Barbecue spice rub, paprika-based

- Season beef generously with yellow mustard and barbecue spice rub.
- Place beef broth in a roasting pan and put the seasoned beef.
- Preheat smoker to 225 F.
- Put beef on the smoker. Smoke for about 3 hours or until temperature reaches 135 F.
- Remove beef from the smoker. Cover with aluminum foil. Let it cool for 10 minutes.
- Slice thinly and serve.

Per Serving: Calories: 354; Total Fat: 16g; Saturated Fat: 6g; Protein: 48g; Carbs: 2g; Fiber: 0g; Sugar: 0g

Montreal Smoked Meat

Serves: 12 / Preparation time: 15 minutes / Cooking time: 8 hours

Montreal smoked meat is a type of meat dish made by salting and curing beef brisket with spices. This is commonly served with French fries, cheese curds and gravy. Bon appetit!

1 whole brisket, 14 pounds, fat cap trimmed to 1/8 inch

For the cure:

1 cup kosher salt

3 tablespoons ground black pepper

3 tablespoons ground coriander

1 tablespoon pink salt

1 tablespoon sugar

1 teaspoon ground bay leaf

1 teaspoon ground cloves

For the rub:

3 tablespoons coarsely ground black pepper

1 tablespoon garlic powder

1 tablespoon ground coriander

1 tablespoon onion powder

1 tablespoon paprika

1 teaspoon celery seed

1 teaspoon dill weed

1 teaspoon ground mustard

1 teaspoon red pepper, crushed

- Combine cure ingredients. Mix thoroughly.
- Season beef generously with the cure mixture.
- Put in a resealable plastic bag. Put in the fridge for 4 days.
- Wash off beef in running water. Soak in water for 2 hours. Pat dry.
- Combine rub ingredients. Mix thoroughly.
- Season beef generously with the rub mixture.
- Preheat smoker to 225 F.
- Put beef on the smoker. Smoke for about 6 hours or until temperature reaches 165 F.
- Put beef in a roasting pan with 1-inch water. Cover and steam beef for 2 hours.
- Put beef in a chopping board. Let cool for a few minutes.
- Slice and serve.

Per Serving: Calories: 704; Total Fat: 33g; Saturated Fat: 12g; Protein: 94g; Carbs: 3g; Fiber: 1g; Sugar: 0g

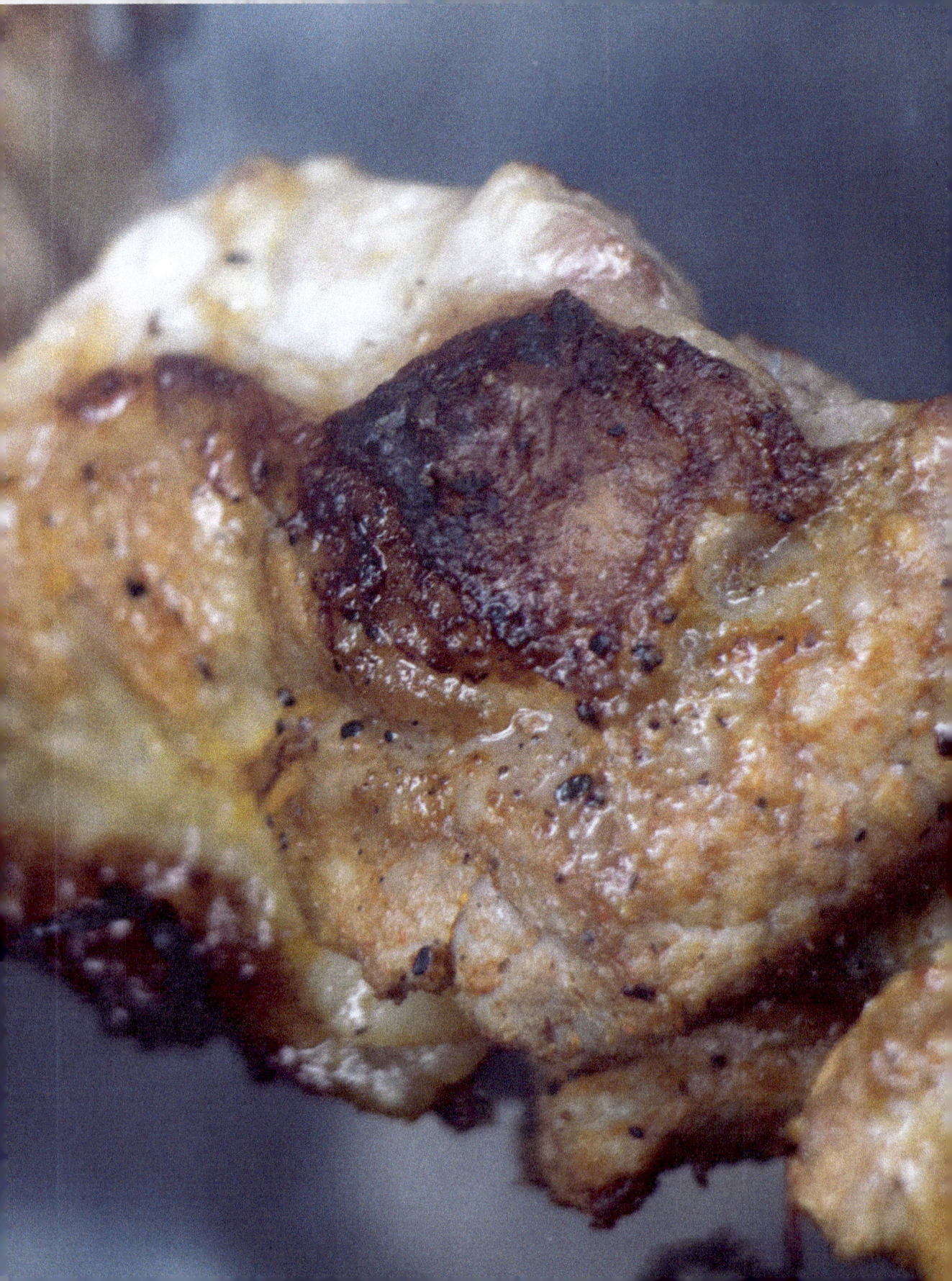

Poultry Recipes

Contents

Whole Smoked Chicken 68

Lemon-Brined Smoked Chicken 69

Smoked Buffalo Chicken Wings 70

Beer Can Chicken 71

Applewood Smoked Chicken 72

Cajun Smoked Chicken Wings 73

Hickory Smoked Chicken 74

Smoked Butter Injected Chicken 75

Smoked Chicken Salad 76

Smoked Bacon Wrapped Chicken Breasts 77

Whole Smoked Chicken

Serves: 8 / Preparation time: 10 minutes / Cooking time: 3 ½ hours

Smoking a whole chicken is long but satisfying. Brining the chicken avoids the meat drying out due to the long cooking time.

5 pounds chicken

1 lemon

1 medium yellow onion

3 whole fresh garlic cloves

5 thyme sprigs

For the rub:

1 tablespoon garlic, crushed

1 teaspoon onion powder

1 teaspoon pepper

1 teaspoon salt

For the brine:

1 gallon water

1 cup brown sugar

½ cup kosher salt

- For the brine, dissolve sugar and salt in 1 gallon water.
- Soak chicken in the brine and put in the fridge overnight.
- Preheat smoker to 225 F.
- Remove chicken from the brine and pat dry.
- Stuff the chicken pouch with lemon, onion, garlic and thyme. Tie the chicken legs together.
- Put chicken on the smoker and smoke for about 3 hours or until temperature reaches 160 F.
- Remove chicken from the smoker. Let it cool for 20 minutes.

Per Serving: Calories: 600; Total Fat: 25g; Saturated Fat: 10g; Protein: 80g; Carbs: 5g; Fiber: 3g; Sugar: 3g

Lemon-Brined Smoked Chicken

Serves: 8 / Preparation time: 30 minutes / Cooking time: 2 ½ hours

Lemon brine helps keep chicken juicy throughout the smoking process. It also helps in the absorption of the salt and seasonings.

2 pieces 4-pound chickens, no backbones and split through the breast

¼ cup spice rub

For the brine:

10 cups water

¾ cups fresh lemon juice

¾ cups kosher salt

2 tablespoons hot sauce

2 teaspoons ground black pepper

2 teaspoons poultry seasoning

- Combine brine ingredients in a saucepan. Bring to a boil. Let it cool.
- Put chicken halves in resealable plastic bags. Pour half of the brine on each bag and seal. Put in the fridge for 8 hours.
- Remove chicken from the brine and pat dry.
- Season chicken generously with the spice rub.
- Preheat smoker to 250 F.
- Put chicken on the smoker. Smoke for about 1 hour or until skin is crisp.
- Turn the chicken to the other side. Smoke for about 1 ½ hours or until temperature reaches 165 F.
- Remove chicken from the smoker. Let it cool for 10 minutes.

Per Serving: Calories: 503; Total Fat: 12g; Saturated Fat: 3g; Protein: 92g; Carbs: 3g; Fiber: 0g; Sugar: 1g

Smoked Buffalo Chicken Wings

Serves: 6 / Preparation time: 30 minutes / Cooking time: 1 ½ hours

Buffalo chicken wings are a favorite party food. Serve with blue cheese or ranch dressing and sliced celery.

18 chicken wings

For the rub:

1 tablespoon olive oil

1 tablespoon pepper

1 tablespoon salt

For the sauce:

1 cup hot sauce

2 tablespoons butter

- Rinse wings in cold water. Pat dry.
- Place in a drying rack and put in the fridge for 3 hours.
- Preheat smoker to 225 F.
- Combine rub ingredients. Mix thoroughly.
- Season chicken generously with the rub.
- Put chicken on the smoker. Smoke for about 1 hour.
- Increase heat to 225 F. Smoke for 30 minutes.
- Remove chicken from the smoker. Mix with the sauce immediately.

Per Serving: Calories: 243; Total Fat: 15g; Saturated Fat: 6g; Protein: 21g; Carbs: 2g; Fiber: 0g; Sugar: 1g

Beer Can Chicken

Serves: 4 / Preparation time: 10 minutes / Cooking time: 1 ½ hours

Beer is not just used for drinking but also for cooking. The beer gives added juiciness and flavor to the chicken.

3 pounds whole chicken

½ can beer

For the rub:

1/3 cup brown sugar

2 tablespoons chili powder

2 tablespoons dry mustard

2 tablespoons paprika

½ teaspoon salt

¼ teaspoon ground black pepper

- Preheat smoker to 375 F.
- Combine rub ingredients. Mix thoroughly.
- Place the half-full can beer at the center of the plate.
- Rinse chicken in cold water. Pat dry.
- Fit chicken over the can of beer with legs at the bottom.
- Season chicken generously with the rub.
- Put the chicken, upright and standing on the can, on the smoker. Smoke for about 1 hour and 15 minutes or until temperature reaches 180 F.
- Remove chicken from the smoker. Discard the beer can.
- Wrap chicken in aluminum foil. Let it cool for 10 minutes.
- Slice and serve.

Per Serving: Calories: 259; Total Fat: 11g; Saturated Fat: 3g; Protein: 42g; Carbs: 18g; Fiber: 0g; Sugar: 17g

Applewood Smoked Chicken

Serves: 6 / Preparation time: 15 minutes / Cooking time: 5 hours

Marinating the chicken in the rub overnight makes a big difference in the way it tastes. Applewood chunks give the chicken a subtle smoky apple flavor.

3 ½ pounds whole chicken

For the rub:

¼ cup dark brown sugar

2 tablespoons chili powder

1 tablespoon garlic powder

1 tablespoon onion powder

1 tablespoon oregano

1 tablespoon smoked paprika

1 teaspoon salt

- Cut the chicken down the middle of the breast.
- Remove all the inside parts from the chicken.
- Rinse chicken in cold water. Pat dry.
- Combine rub ingredients. Mix thoroughly.
- Season chicken generously with the rub.
- Wrap chicken and put in the fridge overnight.
- Preheat smoker to 225 F.
- Put chicken on the smoker and smoke for about 5 hours or until temperature reaches 165 F.
- Remove chicken from the smoker. Let it cool for 10 minutes.
- Slice and serve.

Per Serving: Calories: 374; Total Fat: 8g; Saturated Fat: 2g; Protein: 70g; Carbs: 8g; Fiber: 0g; Sugar: 8g

Cajun Smoked Chicken Wings

Serves: 8 / Preparation time: 20 minutes / Cooking time: 1 hour 20 minutes

Smoky, sweet and sticky, these Cajun Smoked Chicken Wings are very good. This ain't just the same old chicken wings you're already used to.

3 pounds chicken wings

For the rub:

1 tablespoon baking powder

1 teaspoon paprika

½ teaspoon dried thyme

½ teaspoon garlic powder

½ teaspoon onion powder

¼ teaspoon black pepper

¼ teaspoon cumin

¼ teaspoon dried oregano

¼ teaspoon kosher salt

1/8 teaspoon cayenne pepper

For the sauce:

¼ cup butter

¼ cup hot sauce

1 tablespoon Worcestershire sauce

2 tablespoons butter

- Combine rub ingredients. Mix thoroughly.
- Rinse wings in cold water. Pat dry.
- Season chicken generously with the rub.
- Place in a baking sheet and put in the fridge overnight.
- Preheat smoker for 15 minutes.
- Put chicken on the smoker. Smoke for about 30 minutes.
- Increase heat to 350 F. Smoke for 50 minutes.
- Remove chicken from the smoker. Mix with the sauce immediately.
- Serve immediately.

Per Serving: Calories: 274; Total Fat: 11g; Saturated Fat: 3g; Protein: 41g; Carbs: 6g; Fiber: 0g; Sugar: 3g

Hickory Smoked Chicken

Serves: 6 / Preparation time: 30 minutes / Cooking time: 2 hours

Hickory wood chips add the smoky flavor to the chicken. Serve with white barbecue sauce.

6 whole chicken legs, bone-in, skin-on

2 cups white barbecue sauce

For the rub:

1/3 cup vegetable oil

Ground black pepper

Kosher salt

- Rinse chicken in cold water. Pat dry.
- Preheat smoker to 250 F.
- Combine rub ingredients. Mix thoroughly.
- Season chicken generously with the rub.
- Put chicken on the smoker. Smoke for about 30 minutes.
- Rotate chicken. Smoke for another 45 minutes or until temperature reaches 170 F.
- Remove chicken from the smoker. Mix with the sauce immediately.

Per Serving: Calories: 490; Total Fat: 31g; Saturated Fat: 9g; Protein: 50g; Carbs: 38g; Fiber: 0g; Sugar: 30g

Smoked Butter Injected Chicken

Serves: 6 / Preparation time: 10 minutes / Cooking time: 2 hours

Injecting the chicken prior to smoking keeps the meat from drying out due to long cooking. Aside from moisture, injecting a chicken packs it with full flavor.

1 whole chicken

½ stick salted butter

3 tablespoons creole seasoning

- Mix butter with 1 tablespoon creole seasoning. Mix thoroughly.
- Inject chicken with the mixture.
- Season chicken generously with 2 tablespoons creole seasoning.
- Preheat smoker to 350 F.
- Put chicken on the smoker. Smoke until temperature reaches 165 F.
- Remove chicken from the smoker. Let it cool for 30 minutes.

Per Serving: Calories: 516; Total Fat: 16g; Saturated Fat: 6g; Protein: 86g; Carbs: 1g; Fiber: 0g; Sugar: 0g

Smoked Chicken Salad

Serves: 4 / Preparation time: 10 minutes / Cooking time: 2 hours

Smoked chicken adds protein to the salad and transforms it into a full, hearty meal. It also gives great texture and flavor.

1 whole chicken, halved

¼ cup barbecue rub

Salt and pepper, to taste

For the dressing:

¾ cup celery, finely chopped

½ cup mayonnaise

1/3 cup scallions, finely sliced

1 tablespoon freshly squeezed lemon juice

1 tablespoon apple cider vinegar

1 teaspoon hot sauce

1 teaspoon smoked paprika

½ teaspoon celery seeds

- Season chicken generously with barbecue rub.
- Preheat smoker to 225 F.
- Smoke chicken for 2 hours or until temperature reaches 160 F.
- Remove chicken from the smoker. Let it cool for 1 hour.
- Combine dressing ingredients. Mix thoroughly.
- Pull chicken meat and chop. Put in bowl and add dressing.
- Mix, season with salt and pepper.
- Serve immediately.

Per Serving: Calories: 438; Total Fat: 27g; Saturated Fat: 8g; Protein: 40g; Carbs: 5g; Fiber: 3g; Sugar: 2g

Smoked Bacon Wrapped Chicken Breasts

Serves: 6 / Preparation time: 30 minutes / Cooking time: 5 hours

This recipe is easy to prepare. Bacon adds flavor to the chicken breasts.

6 chicken breasts, boneless and skinless

18 slices regular cut bacon

Chicken rub

Barbecue sauce

For the brine:

4 cups water

¼ cup brown sugar

¼ cup kosher salt

- Combine brine ingredients. Mix thoroughly.
- Soak chicken on the brine mixture. Put in the fridge for 2 hours.
- Rinse chicken in cold water. Pat dry.
- Season chicken with the rub.
- Wrap each chicken with 3 strips of bacon. Secure with toothpick.
- Preheat smoker to 230 F.
- Put chicken on the smoker and smoke for about 3 hours or until temperature reaches 165 F.
- Glaze with barbecue sauce 30 minutes before finishing.
- Remove chicken from the smoker. Let it cool and serve.

Per Serving: Calories: 289; Total Fat: 20g; Saturated Fat: 6g; Protein: 27g; Carbs: 13g; Fiber: 0g; Sugar: 6g

Seafood Recipes

Contents

Smoked Crab Legs 80

Bacon Wrapped Smoked Shrimp 81

Smoked Shrimp Kabobs... 82

Cedar Plank Smoked Tuna Steak........................... 83

Lemon Smoked Tuna 84

Smoked Lobster Tails... 85

Cedar Plank Smoked Salmon 86

Bacon Wrapped Smoked Scallops.......................... 87

Smoked Trout 88

Cajun Smoked Catfish.. 89

Smoked Crab Legs

Serves: 6 / Preparation time: 15 minutes / Cooking time: 30 minutes

Smoked crab legs are easy to prepare and cook. Serve with cocktail sauce.

3 pounds crab legs, thawed

1 cup butter, melted

2 tablespoon lemon juice, freshly-squeezed

1 tablespoon Cajun rub

2 cloves garlic, minced

- Put crab legs in a roasting pan.
- Mix butter, lemon juice and garlic. Mix thoroughly.
- Pour over mixture to the crab legs.
- Season with Cajun rub.
- Preheat smoker to 350 F.
- Put crab legs on the smoker. Smoke for 30 minutes.
- Remove crab legs from the smoker. Serve with the sauce.

Per Serving: Calories: 245; Total Fat: 8g; Saturated Fat: 1g; Protein: 23g; Carbs: 5g; Fiber: 0g; Sugar: 6g

Bacon Wrapped Smoked Shrimp

Serves: 8 / Preparation time: 5 minutes / Cooking time: 20 minutes

This recipe can be prepared during holidays and doesn't take much time. It's a favorite dish for the young and old.

1 ½ pounds jumbo shrimp, cleaned

10 strips bacon

For the marinade:

¼ cup olive oil

2 tablespoon fresh lemon juice

1 tablespoon lemon zest

1 teaspoon clove garlic, minced

1 teaspoon fresh parsley, chopped

1 teaspoon salt

½ teaspoon pepper

- Rinse shrimp in cold water. Pat dry. Place in a bowl.
- Combine marinade ingredients. Place in a small jar with tight lid and shake vigorously.
- Soak shrimp in the mixture. Put in the fridge for 1 hour.
- Preheat smoker to 400 F.
- Smoke bacon strips for 12 minutes.
- Drain the shrimp. Wrap each shrimp with bacon strip. Secure with a toothpick.
- Smoke for 4 minutes on each side.
- Remove shrimp from the smoker. Serve immediately.

Per Serving: Calories: 275; Total Fat: 16g; Saturated Fat: 5g; Protein: 16g; Carbs: 5g; Fiber: 1g; Sugar: 4g

Smoked Shrimp Kabobs

Serves: 4 / Preparation time: 5 minutes / Cooking time: 35 minutes

Smoked Shrimp Kabobs are easy to prepare and enjoy. Smoke flavor blends well with the shrimp.

1 ½ pounds large shrimp

½ cup olive oil

For the rub:

6 garlic cloves, finely chopped

2 tablespoons parsley, finely chopped

½ teaspoon black pepper

½ teaspoon cayenne pepper

½ teaspoon salt

- Combine rub ingredients. Mix thoroughly.
- Season shrimp generously with the rub on all sides. Let sit for 20 minutes.
- Sprinkle olive oil on the shrimp.
- Skewer shrimp on a kabob.
- Preheat smoker to 225 F.
- Smoke shrimp kabobs for 35 minutes.
- Remove shrimp from the smoker. Serve immediately.

Per Serving: Calories: 90; Total Fat: 4g; Saturated Fat: 1g; Protein: 16g; Carbs: 2g; Fiber: 1g; Sugar: 0g

Cedar Plank Smoked Tuna Steak

Serves: 4 / Preparation time: 5 minutes / Cooking time: 15 minutes

This smoked tuna steak recipe has an Asian flare. Use cedar plank when smoking for added flavor.

4 pieces 6 ounces fresh tuna steaks, 1-inch thick

4 bunches baby bok choy

2 teaspoons sesame seeds, toasted

For the marinade:

2 tablespoons rice vinegar

2 tablespoons green onion, finely chopped

1 tablespoon fresh cilantro, snipped

1 tablespoon fresh ginger, grated

1 tablespoon lime juice

1 tablespoon sesame oil, toasted

2 teaspoons soy-sauce

½ teaspoon lime peel, finely shredded

¼ teaspoon salt

¼ teaspoon red pepper, crushed

1 clove garlic, minced

- Rinse fish in cold water. Pat dry.
- Combine marinade ingredients in a shallow disk. Set aside ¼ cup of the marinade.
- Soak fish in the mixture. Put in the fridge for 1 hour.
- Drain the fish. Slice bok choy bunches in halves lengthwise. Set aside.
- Preheat smoker for 3 minutes.
- Smoke tuna steaks for 15 minutes.
- Smoke bok choy for 3 minutes.
- Remove tuna and bok choy from the smoker.
- Sprinkle bok choy with the remaining marinade.
- Drizzle bok choy and tuna with sesame seeds.

Per Serving: Calories: 86; Total Fat: 5g; Saturated Fat: 2g; Protein: 11g; Carbs: 0g; Fiber: 3g; Sugar: 0g

Lemon Smoked Tuna

Serves: 4 / Preparation time: 5 minutes / Cooking time: 1 hour and 45 minutes

This recipe is made with Ahi tuna steak, but you can substitute it with yellow fin tuna steak. Lemon brings out the natural flavor of fish.

4 Ahi tuna steaks

1 lemon, sliced

For the rub:

2 tablespoons garlic, minced

2 tablespoons lemon juice

2 tablespoons lemon pepper seasoning

2 tablespoons olive oil

Salt and pepper

- Combine rub ingredients. Mix thoroughly.
- Season tuna steaks generously with the rub on all sides. Put a slice of lemon on each tuna steak. Place tuna over ice.
- Preheat smoker to 190 F.
- Smoke tuna steaks for 1 hour and 45 minutes or until temperature reaches 145 F.
- Remove shrimp from the smoker. Garnish with freshly sliced lemon.

Per Serving: Calories: 267; Total Fat: 21g; Saturated Fat: 3g; Protein: 20g; Carbs: 1g; Fiber: 0g; Sugar: 1g

Smoked Lobster Tails

Serves: 6 / Preparation time: 10 minutes / Cooking time: 20 minutes

Lobsters are mostly cooked in a pot of boiling water but smoking a lobster provides a bold flavor that boiling can't give. It is very easy to prepare.

6 lobster tails   4 cloves garlic

¼ cup butter

- Preheat smoker to 400 F.
- Open lobster tails and release meat from inside of shell using your finger.
- Mix butter and garlic over medium-low heat.
- Drizzle mixture over lobster meat in the opened shell.
- Smoke lobster tails until temperature reaches 145 F.
- Remove lobster tails from the smoker. Let sit for a few minutes.
- Lift out lobster meat using a fork.
- Serve with garlic butter.

Per Serving: Calories: 90; Total Fat: 3g; Saturated Fat: 2g; Protein: 20g; Carbs: 0g; Fiber: 0g; Sugar: 0g

Cedar Plank Smoked Salmon

Serves: 6 / Preparation time: 10 minutes / Cooking time: 20 minutes

Use cedar plank when smoking for added flavor. Serve with Asian-inspired rice and roasted asparagus.

1-pound wild salmon fillet, skin-on, center-cut

2 slices lemon

4 sprigs thyme

For the brine:

4 cups water

¾ cup light brown sugar

½ cup kosher salt

Freshly ground pepper

- Combine brine ingredients in a bowl. Mix thoroughly.
- Soak salmon in the mixture. Cover and put in the fridge overnight.
- Drain the salmon and pat dry. Season with salt and pepper.
- Layer with lemon slices and thyme sprigs.
- Preheat smoker to 250 F.
- Smoke salmon for 20 minutes.
- Remove salmon from the smoker. Serve hot.

Per Serving: Calories: 100; Total Fat: 4g; Saturated Fat: 1g; Protein: 16g; Carbs: 2g; Fiber: 1g; Sugar: 1g

Bacon Wrapped Smoked Scallops

Serves: 12 / Preparation time: 10 minutes / Cooking time: 20 minutes

This is a great appetizer that can be served on any occasion. Serve with seafood sauce.

24 jumbo deep-sea scallops, dry-packed

12 slices bacon, thinly cut in half crosswise

½ cup butter

1 clove garlic, minced

Salt and pepper, as needed

- Dry scallops on paper towels. Put in a bowl.
- Mix butter and garlic in a saucepan. Cook for 1 minute. Let cool.
- Pour mixture over the scallops.
- Season scallops with salt and pepper.
- Wrap a piece of bacon on each scallop. Secure with a toothpick.
- Preheat smoker to 400 F.
- Smoke scallops for 20 minutes.
- Remove scallops from the smoker.
- Put in a platter and serve with lemon wedges.

Per Serving: Calories: 162; Total Fat: 12g; Saturated Fat: 6g; Protein: 12g; Carbs: 0g; Fiber: 0g; Sugar: 0g

Smoked Trout

Serves: 8 / Preparation time: 5 minutes / Cooking time: 2 hours

Smoked trout is an easy and quick meal. It is also a perfect ingredient for sandwiches and dips.

8 rainbow trout

For the brine:

1-gallon water

½ cup brown sugar

¼ cup salt

2 tablespoon soy sauce

1 tablespoon black pepper

- Combine brine ingredients. Mix thoroughly.
- Soak fish in the brine for 1 hour.
- Preheat smoker to 225 F.
- Drain fish and pat dry.
- Smoke fish for the 2 hours.
- Remove fish from the smoker. Serve hot.

Per Serving: Calories: 117; Total Fat: 4g; Saturated Fat: 1g; Protein: 18g; Carbs: 1g; Fiber: 0g; Sugar: 1g

Cajun Smoked Catfish

Serves: 8 / Preparation time: 10 minutes / Cooking time: 2 ½ hours

This recipe is designed to enhance the flavor of the catfish. It's tender, moist and full of flavor.

8 catfish fillets

Water

1 cup hot sauce

1 cup salt

Cajun seasoning

Salt and black pepper

- Prepare brine by putting half full water and ½ cup salt in casserole dishes.
- Soak catfish in the dishes. Put in the fridge for 4 hours.
- Preheat smoker to 200 F.
- Drain fish and pat dry.
- Sprinkle catfish with Cajun seasoning, salt and pepper.   Top with hot sauce.
- Smoke fish for the 2 ½ hours.
- Remove fish from the smoker. Let it sit for 15 minutes.

Per Serving: Calories: 139; Total Fat: 5g; Saturated Fat: 1g; Protein: 21g; Carbs: 0g; Fiber: 0g; Sugar: 0g

The "Dirty Dozen" and "Clean 15"

Lots of folks love eating some fruits and veggies on the side with their smoked meat. These sides are often healthy, but sometimes looks can be deceiving. Every year, the Environmental Working Group releases a list of the produce with the most pesticide residue (Dirty Dozen) and a list of the ones with the least chance of having residue (Clean 15). It's based on analysis from the U.S. Department of Agriculture Pesticide Data Program report.

The Environmental Working Group found that 70% of the 48 types of produce tested had residues of at least one type of pesticide. In total there were 178 different pesticides and pesticide breakdown products. This residue can stay on veggies and fruit even after they are washed and peeled. All pesticides are toxic to humans and consuming them can cause damage to the nervous system, reproductive system, cancer, a weakened immune system, and more. Women who are pregnant can expose their unborn children to toxins through their diet, and continued exposure to pesticides can affect their development.

This info can help you choose the best fruits and veggies, as well as which ones you should always try to buy organic.

THE DIRTY DOZEN

- Strawberries
- Spinach
- Nectarines
- Apples
- Peaches
- Celery
- Grapes
- Pears
- Cherries
- Tomatoes
- Sweet bell peppers
- Potatoes

THE CLEAN 15

- Sweet corn
- Avocados
- Pineapples
- Cabbage
- Onions
- Frozen sweet peas
- Papayas
- Asparagus
- Mangoes
- Eggplant
- Honeydew
- Kiwi
- Cantaloupe
- Cauliflower
- Grapefruit

Measurement Conversion Tables

Volume Equivalents (Liquid)

US Standard	US Standard (ounces)	Metric (Approx.)
2 tablespoons	1 fl oz	30 ml
¼ cup	2 fl oz	60 ml
½ cup	4 fl oz	120 ml
1 cup	8 fl oz	240 ml
1 ½ cups	12 fl oz	355 ml
2 cups or 1 pint	16 fl oz	475 ml
4 cups or 1 quart	32 fl oz	1 L
1 gallon	128 fl oz	4 L

Oven Temperatures

Fahrenheit (F)	Celsius (C) (Approx)
250 F	120 C
300 F	150 C
325 F	165 C
350 F	180 C
375 F	190 C
400 F	200 C
425 F	220 C
450 F	230 C

Volume Equivalents (Dry)

US Standard	Metric (Approx.)
¼ teaspoon	1 ml
½ teaspoon	2 ml
1 teaspoon	5 ml
1 tablespoon	15 ml
¼ cup	59 ml
½ cup	118 ml
1 cup	235 ml

Weight Equivalents

US Standard	Metric (Approx.)
½ ounce	15 g
1 ounce	30 g
2 ounces	60 g
4 ounces	115 g
8 ounces	225 g
12 ounces	340 g
16 ounces or 1 pound	455 g

Recipe Index

A
Andouille Sausage, 39
Applewood Smoked Chicken, 72

B
Bacon Wrapped Chicken Breasts, 77
Bacon Wrapped Smoked Scallops, 87
Bacon Wrapped Smoked Shrimp, 81
Beef Brisket (Texas Style), 53
Beef Burnt Ends, 58
Beef Chuck, 52
Beef Jerky, 56
Beef Ribs, 54
Beef Rump Roast, 64
Beef Sandwich, 63
Beef Stew, 55
Beef Tenderloin, 59
Beer Can Chicken, 71
Buffalo Chicken Wings, 70
Butter Injected Chicken, 75

C
Cajun Smoked Catfish, 89
Cajun Smoked Chicken Wings, 73
Caramelized Onion Burgers, 61
Cedar Plank Smoked Salmon, 86
Cedar Plank Smoked Tuna Steak, 83
Chicken Salad, 76
Crab Legs, 80

G
Grass-Fed Beef Sirloin Kebabs, 60

H

Ham and Cheese Fatty, 40
Hickory Smoked Chicken, 74
Homemade Bacon, 45
Honey Glazed Smoked Ham, 46

I

Italian Sausage, 41

K

Kielbasa, 42

L

Lemon Smoked Tuna, 84
Lemon-Brined Smoked Chicken, 69
Lobster Tails, 85

M

Montreal Smoked Meat, 65

P

Pork (Perfect Smoked), 49
Pork Belly, 34
Pork Butt, 48
Pork Chops, 35
Pork Shoulder, 36
Pork Tenderloin, 37
Pulled Beef, 62
Pulled Pork, 47

R

Ribs with Chipotle and Lime, 38
Ribs, 43
Roast Beef, 57

S

Salsa Fatty Meatloaf, 44

Shrimp Kabobs, 82

T

Trout, 88

W

Whole Smoked Chicken, 68

Would you like a healthy salad with that?

Enjoy a full week of fresh, healthy salad recipes. A new salad for every day of the week!

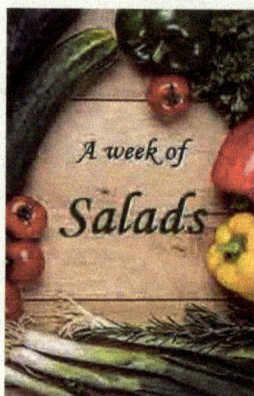

Grab this bonus recipe ebook *free* as our gift to you:

http://salad7.hotbooks.org

Want MORE full length cookbooks for FREE?

We invite you to sign up for free review copies of future books!

Learn more and get brand new cookbooks for *free*:

http://club.hotbooks.org

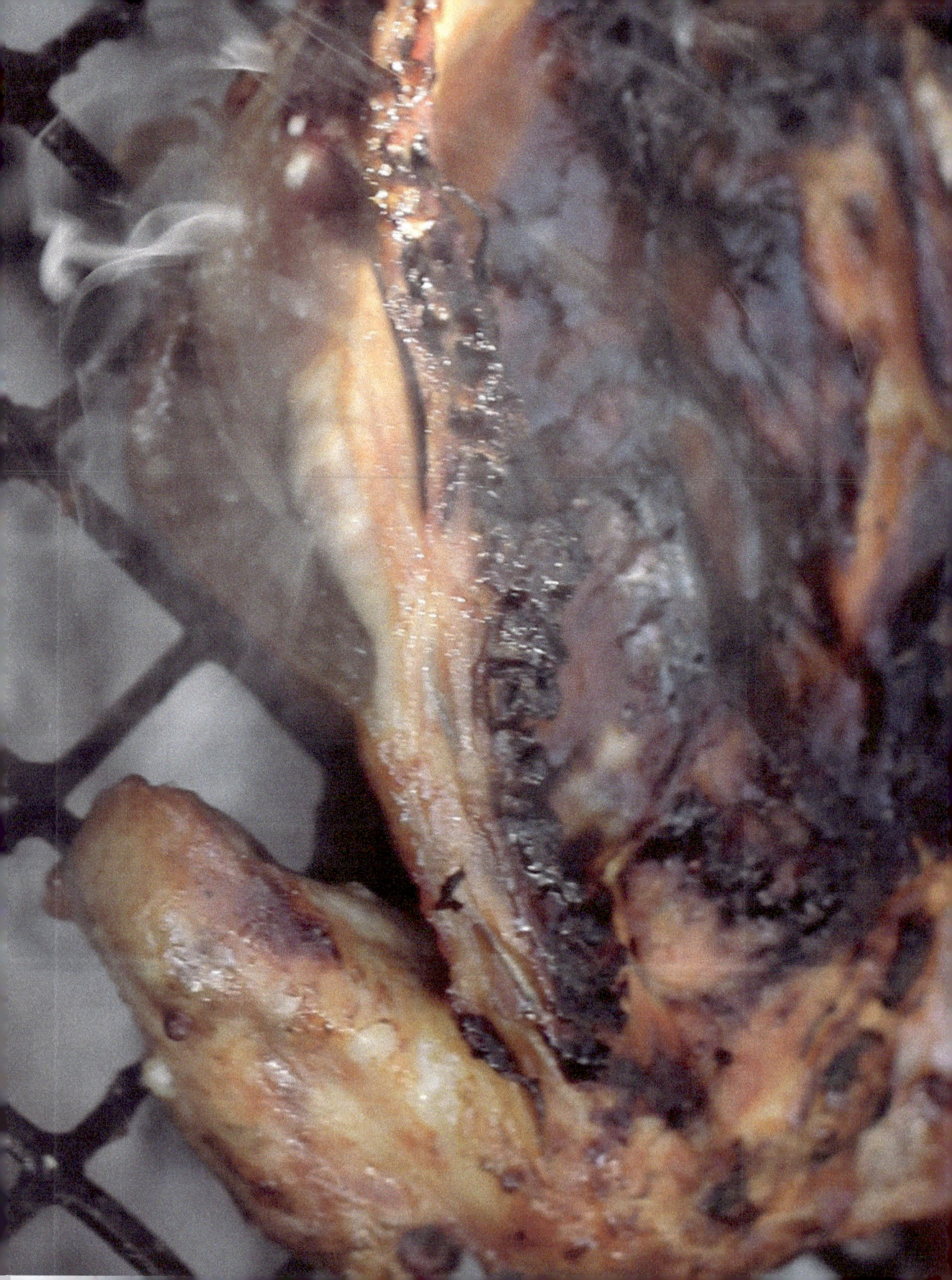

Well, that's it. That's all she wrote. Or all I wrote, at least. I really hope you and your folks found the information in this cookbook to be helpful and the recipes to be a tasty way to enjoy cooking on your electric smoker. Now that you've made it to the end, I would really appreciate if you would share your opinion with me by writing a review on Amazon. I take the time to read every single one of them and I always love to hear from a fellow local "pitmaster". Please take a moment and share your valued feedback with me.

Happy smoking!
Hank Dunn